ALL THINGS NEW

A DISCIPLESHIP MINISTRY FOR LIFE TRANSFORMATION

FACILITATOR GUIDE

All Things New: A Discipleship Ministry for Life Transformation
All Things New Facilitator Guide

ISBN : 978-1-943852-96-3

Printed in the United States of America.

Copyright © 2018 by Debora Barr
DBarrMinistries@gmail.com
www.DBarrMinistries.org

True Potential, Inc.
PO Box 904
Travelers Rest, SC 29690
www.truepotentialmedia.com

True Potential
REACH THE WORLD

Contents

ABOUT THE AUTHOR

The All Things New Ministry was born out of my transition out of nearly two decades of homosexuality through the love and support of a women's ministry Bible study group and the leadership of a church that was not willing to compromise their convictions while continuing to welcome and embrace me. If homosexuality is not your life-controlling issue, please know that this Discipleship Ministry will help you just like it helped me! God's Word changes lives no matter what areas of brokenness you have in your life! When I first began attending the church that started the transformation in my life, I had not yet accepted Jesus Christ as my Lord and Savior and I was happy living my life as a lesbian. I knew 'about' Jesus and what He did for me, and even labeled myself as a Christian, but I had not yet surrendered my whole life to Him. I had also been involved in a gay church for many years where I was indoctrinated in gay-theology, which affirmed my lifestyle as a part of the gay community. I was still living my life the way I wanted to, and that included being in a committed lesbian relationship with the woman I loved.

Once I fully surrendered my life to Jesus Christ, I began to regularly read the Bible and pray that God would reveal areas of sin in my life that I needed to repent of and turn away from. It was through my study of the Word of God that I realized that many areas of my life did not line up with His Word. As God revealed areas of sin, I repented and asked for his forgiveness, and He began to change me from the inside out. Only when the Scriptures guide your conduct, does transformation begin in your life. When I finally realized that God did not approve of my choice to live as a lesbian, I decided to turn away from homosexuality and live a life in a way that was pleasing to Him. The transition was not easy, and I relied heavily on the women in my Bible study who supported me with unconditional love and prayed for me as I turned away from the gay community, which had been my support structure for many years. I had to walk away from a relationship with the woman that I loved and we had to unravel our lives that we had previously intertwined together.

My prayer is that every person who is disconnected from God will establish an intimate relationship with Jesus Christ that completely transforms their life for all of eternity. His love is everlasting and completely satisfying – it is unlike anything we can ever experience in human relationships. I never knew that I wasn't living my best life until I was able to experience His love as I aligned my life with His Word. Jesus makes all things new!

Therefore, if anyone is in Christ, he is a new creation; old things have passed away; behold, all things have become new. (2 Corinthians 5:17 NKJV)

Contact the author:
Debora Barr
www.DBarrMinistries.org
DBarrMinistries@gmail.com

INTRODUCTION

ALL THINGS NEW: A DISCIPLESHIP MINISTRY FOR HEALING is a Bible Study and Discipleship Ministry for all people who are disconnected from a personal intimate relationship with Jesus Christ and are not experiencing the abundant life that is promised in the Bible to all who surrender their whole lives to the Lordship of Jesus Christ. It is designed to be facilitated by lay leaders who have a heart for God. The purpose of the All Things New Ministry is to aid in the spiritual healing and growth of people who are hungry for life transformation. This ministry is designed to help release people from the bondage of sin and to allow them to experience healing from the effects of having their lives separated or distant from God.

It is important that the ministry leaders create a safe environment for healing; train participants in the Ministry to examine their lives in light of biblical truth; and cultivate personal intimacy with Jesus Christ that leads to true Discipleship. It is important that the ministry leader is able to be transparent about their own struggles with sin, to be honest about their relationship with God, and not pretend to be an expert in spirituality. By being transparent about our struggles with sin, we open up the dialogue and create a safe environment for healing.

Each participant in the discipleship ministry should connect with an Accountability Partner who serves as a mentor/Christian friend to pray for and support the participant as he/she works through the weekly lessons. Accountability Partners are not counselors or therapists; they are mature Christians who have a heart for serving and supporting others who desire to live a holy life and are committed to pray for the person that they are supporting.

The Facilitators and Accountability Partners agree to maintain the confidentiality of all participants in the ministry to provide a safe environment for people to openly discuss their feelings and struggles with sin. All information shared in the group must be kept confidential with limited exceptions, for example, if you believe a participant is at risk for suicide, or if you believe someone intends to harm another person, they need to be connected with professionals who can further help them.

OTHER RESOURCES FOR COMPLETION OF THIS COURSE

It is recommended that the facilitator obtain a copy of *A Guide for Listening and Inner Healing Prayer: Meeting God in the Broken Places* by Rusty Rustenbach (NavPress 2011) ISBN: 978-1-61747-086-8 – used for Lesson #15 – Listening and Inner Healing Prayer.

This book walks you through the process of learning to listen to God for healing in prayer and was used by the author to develop this lesson. The second half of the book can be used by a facilitator to guide others through Listening and Inner Healing Prayer. A link to purchase this book and other resources to help facilitate Listening prayer can be found on Debora's website at http://www.DBarrMinistries.org

For the lesson on Spiritual Gifts and Calling (Lesson #19 on page 84), you will need to provide participants with a Spiritual Gifts Inventory Assessment tool. These can be found by searching the Internet or by visiting a Christian bookstore.

SCHEDULING

The in-class meetings are designed for a two-hour time block.

A typical weekly Bible Study class consists of:

- 5 minutes – Scripture Memory Quiz/Demonstration
- 10 minutes – Praise and Worship followed by Prayer *(assign a participant to serve as Worship/ Prayer Leader for each class)*
- 30 minutes – Break Down the Memory Verse and Homework Discussion
- 60 - 70 minutes – Weekly Lesson
- 5 minutes – Closing Prayer

Visit Debora's Website for links to current information and resources: www.DBarrMinistries.org/

WEEKLY HOMEWORK

Each in-class lesson is preceded by a week of homework that needs to be completed by each participant (and ministry leader) prior to meeting as a group. Each homework assignment consists of five days' worth of individual Bible study plus a Scripture that relates to the week's lesson and is to be memorized by each person. Scripture memory is demonstrated by either asking participants to recite Scripture from memory, or write it out and turn it in at the beginning of the class.

ACCOUNTABILITY PARTNERS

The Accountability Partner serves as a Christian mentor/friend to a person who is completing this Discipleship Ministry program. Their role is to encourage and provide unconditional love and a listening ear to a person who is trying to live a life pleasing to God. They should have a heart for hurting people and an ability to listen and continually point a person to Jesus for the deliverance and healing necessary to overcome the effects of sin. They should also pray regularly for the person they are paired with.

Each person that is interested in serving in this ministry should be screened by the ministry leaders prior to pairing them with a participant. There is a sample Accountability Partner Application in the FORMS section at the end of this Facilitator Guide that you can use for this purpose. It is important that each potential applicant has the right motives and a true heart for serving in this capacity, which has been demonstrated by their participation and service in other areas of ministry. It would be quite harmful to have a person serving as an Accountability Partner who is judgmental and condescending towards a person who struggles with sin, or who has some negative ulterior motive for wanting to serve in this capacity. All efforts must be made by the ministry leaders to create a safe environment for each of the participants in the ministry.

SAMPLE FORMS

Sample Forms are provided in the back of this Facilitator Guide for the administration and evaluation of this ministry.

HOW TO USE THIS FACILITATOR GUIDE

Each lesson plan in this facilitator's guide directly corresponds with the weekly homework assignments in the participant workbook. For example, Lesson #1 homework is to be completed by the participants prior to coming together as a class for discussion of Lesson #1.

The basic format for each lesson plan is as follows:

1. Reproduction of the introductory material for each homework assignment, including the weekly Scripture memory verse
2. Breakdown of the underlined key terms/concepts that make up the memory verse along with some questions to encourage discussion about the Scripture verse
3. Questions to encourage discussion about the homework
4. In-class exercises to include small group activities, and fill in the blank exercises
5. New lesson material that will lead into the next week's homework

For best results, the Group Facilitator should complete the homework and memorize the Scripture along with the participants before coming together to lead the group discussion. The Facilitator also needs to review and become familiar with the weekly Lesson Plan he/she will be using to facilitate the in-class discussions, as it may be necessary to modify the lesson plan to tailor the lesson to each group being served. Also, preparing ahead of time examples and testimonies from the life of the Facilitator related to the lesson will have a greater impact towards opening up discussion among the group than merely relying on the author's testimony.

As you review the Lesson Plans, you will see bulleted italicized text following many of the questions posed by the author. These are points that you should try to draw out of the class during discussion. For lessons that have an in-class exercise, the answers to the puzzles as well as the fill-in-the-blank exercises are provided in the Facilitator's Guide.

Throughout the Facilitator's Guide, you will find Scriptures to reinforce points being made in the lesson. Have a participant read the Scripture that corresponds to the point being made before revealing the answer to the fill-in-the-blank.

Use your imagination as a Facilitator to make each lesson interesting and engaging for the participants. Following are some ideas that you may want to incorporate into the weekly lessons:

- Ask for Testimonies of what God has done in the live of the participants this week
- Ask for Testimonies of what God has revealed to us through His Word this week
- Use worship videos at the beginning of class that correspond to, and reinforce the weekly lesson
- Show video clips to illustrate teaching points from the weekly lesson
- Incorporate comedy or a skit to illustrate a teaching point
- Arts and Crafts that reinforce a lesson
- Assign a person to bring in an illustration or object that reinforces the weekly lesson
- Team-building exercises in class

MINISTRY ORIENTATION MEETING

The orientation meeting is designed to set the expectations for those who have decided to join the ministry, and to ensure each Participant has the necessary materials to begin the first week homework assignment.

TARGET AUDIENCE - Ministry Participants and Potential Accountability Partners.

RESOURCES NEEDED FOR THIS CLASS

- Copies of the workbook used for this Ministry
- Registration Forms for potential Participants and Accountability Partners (located in FORMS section at the back of the Facilitator Guide)
- Copy of the Covenant Statement to be signed by all Participants (located in the FORMS section at the back of the Facilitator Guide)

WELCOME

PRAYER

INTRODUCE MINISTRY FACILITATORS

ICEBREAKER ACTIVITY

Interview someone you don't know and then report to the group the answers provided by the person you interviewed.

- When you were a little boy/girl, what did you want to 'be when you grow up'?
- Did you end up doing what you thought you would as a child?
- What is your most important accomplishment in life so far? What are you most proud of?

Following the icebreaker activity, have each person introduce themselves to the group and state why they are interested in participating in this ministry.

OVERVIEW AND EXPECTATIONS

- This ministry does not provide counseling of any sort
  - □ We are simply sisters/brothers in Christ who are coming alongside you as God helps you to heal from past wounds and help you to connect intimately with Jesus Christ for life transformation.

- Attendance
  - □ Each lesson builds on the previous lesson and it is important that you attend class each week
  - □ If you cannot come to class for any reason, please alert the facilitator

- Homework – weekly lessons with 5 days of homework is in the Workbook
  - ☐ Complete the homework the week prior to meeting with the group.

- Scripture Memorization
  - ☐ written or oral quiz at the beginning of each class

- Accountability Partners will be assigned to each participant in the ministry
  - ☐ The men and women who have expressed an interest in serving in this capacity had to fill out an application to serve in this capacity and will be screened by the ministry leaders prior to being assigned to the participants.

- Prayer
  - ☐ God moves on our behalf when we pray.

- Confidentiality
  - ☐ What is shared in the weekly meetings stays in this ministry. We are here to learn and to heal and to grow spiritually.
  - ☐ We will respect each other's privacy at all times.

HAVE ALL PARTICIPANTS SIGN A COPY OF THE COVENANT STATEMENT
found in the FORMS Section of the Facilitator Guide. Make a copy of the signed document for each participant.

QUESTIONS & ANSWERS

Assign Week #1 Homework

CLOSING PRAYER

Complete and turn in Registration Forms (as necessary)

The Word is Life

FACILITATOR'S GUIDE

RESOURCES NEEDED FOR THIS CLASS

- Lesson #1 In-Class Discussion Fill in the Blank form (available in Workbook and in the ADDITIONAL CLASSROOM MATERIALS FOR INDIVIDUAL LESSONS Section of this Facilitator Guide)

God speaks to us today through his written Word, which has the amazing power to transform your life if you read and study it daily. It is living and powerful and discerns the thoughts and intents of our hearts (Hebrews 4:12-13). It is inspired by God and equips us for the work God has for our lives (2 Timothy 3:16-17). There are numerous Scriptures in the Bible where God tells us about the power of His Word to transform our lives:

Joshua 1:8 - *This Book of the Law shall not depart from your mouth, but you shall meditate in it day and night, that you may observe to do according to all that is written in it. For then you will make your way prosperous, and then you will have good success.*

Jeremiah 23:29 - *"Is not My word like a fire?" says the Lord, "And like a hammer that breaks the rock in pieces?"*

1 Peter 1:23 - *...the word of God ... lives and abides forever.*

1 Thessalonians 2:13 - *For this reason we also thank God without ceasing, because when you received the word of God which you heard from us, you welcomed it not as the word of men, but as it is in truth, the word of God, which also effectively works in you who believe.*

John 17:17 - *Sanctify them by Your truth. Your word is truth.*

Acts 20:32 - *So now, brethren, I commend you to God and to the word of His grace, which is able to build you up and give you an inheritance among all those who are sanctified.*

God's Word makes us prosperous and successful; it breaks up sin in our lives; it lives and abides forever; effectively works in our lives; brings truth; builds us up and gives an eternal inheritance. What awesome power and amazing promises!

We will be walking a journey together through the Word of God to learn how He transforms lives and brings hope and healing to His children who desire to know Him more. God loves you and He demonstrates His love all throughout the Bible, which is His written word of hope for all people. Let's begin our journey together and see what He has in store for you.

This Week's Memory Verse

Psalm 1:2-3 (NKJV) *"But his delight is in the <u>law of the Lord</u>, and in His law he <u>meditates</u> day and night. He shall be like a <u>tree</u> planted by the rivers of water that <u>brings forth its fruit in its season</u>, whose leaf also shall not wither; and whatever he does shall prosper."*

Break Down the Memory Verse *(Definitions from Unger 's Bible Dictionary)*

<u>Law of the Lord</u> – The revealed will of God with respect to human conduct.

<u>Meditate</u> – private devotional act consisting of deliberate reflection on a spiritual truth. It should be deliberate, close, and continuous.

What are the characteristics of a <u>tree</u> planted by rivers of water that can be applied to our lives if we meditate on God's Word day and night?

    ☐   *Healthy and green because the water nourishes the root system and the leaves do not wither.*
    ☐   *We will have a continuous source of nourishment for our spiritual lives.*

What does it mean spiritually for us to <u>bring forth fruit in season</u>?

    ☐   *As we continually meditate on the Word of God, we will mature spiritually and be able to manifest the Fruit of the Spirit (Gal 5:22-23)*

What is the promise associated with this passage? Why do you think that is?

    ☐   *Whatever we do will prosper*
    ☐   *If we align our lives with the will of God (the law), we will prosper in everything we do because God's will and way is perfect*

Questions for Discussion:

- Did you have any challenges completing the daily homework assignment this week? Why/why not?
- Which lesson did you find easiest to finish? Why?
- Which lesson challenged you the most? Why?

Review some of the actual homework questions and encourage sharing by all of the participants.

Fill in the blank Exercise (Located behind this week's homework in the Workbook, and in the appendix to this Facilitator Guide). Or use your imagination as a facilitator to make each lesson interesting and engaging for the participants utilizing some of the ideas presented in the "How to Use This Facilitator Guide" section on page 9.

Bible Facts

1. The <u>66 books</u> of the Bible (<u>39</u> Old Testament and <u>27</u> New Testament) were written:

   • By more than <u>40 men</u> inspired by <u>God</u>
   • Over a period of approximately <u>1600</u> years

The Power of the God's Word to transform lives

2 Timothy 3:16-17 - All Scripture is given by inspiration of God, and is profitable for doctrine, for reproof, for correction, for instruction in righteousness, that the man of God may be complete, thoroughly equipped for every good work.

What does this passage say Scripture is profitable for?

2. Scripture is profitable for <u>Doctrine</u>, <u>Reproof</u>, <u>Correction</u>, and <u>Instruction</u> in righteousness (2 Timothy 3:16-17)

   • *Doctrine – is a principle or body of principles presented for acceptance or belief*
   • *Reproof – is a rebuke, or to voice or convey disapproval*
      ▫ *God teaches us what His will is for our lives through His Word*
      ▫ *Every aspect of human life is revealed in His Word*

Hebrews 4:12-13 - For the word of God is living and powerful, and sharper than any two-edged sword, piercing even to the division of soul and spirit, and of joints and marrow, and is a discerner of the thoughts and intents of the heart. And there is no creature hidden from His sight, but all things are naked and open to the eyes of Him to whom we must give account.

What is this passage revealing to us about God's Word?

3. The Word of God is <u>living</u> and <u>powerful</u> (Hebrews 4:12-13)

      ▫ *It is living – meaning, it is relevant to us today. It is not an old story that doesn't apply to our lives.*
      ▫ *Piercing to the division of soul (mind, will, emotions) and spirit (God's Holy Spirit within us)*

4. The Word of God is a <u>discerner of the</u> <u>thoughts</u> and <u>intents</u> of the heart. (Hebrews 4:12-13)

      ▫ *Discerner of thoughts and intents of the heart – brings conviction because God knows what is in our hearts*

Facilitator should share a personal testimony of how God's Word brought conviction to them, and then ask if others would be willing to share something similar.

God's Word will transform your life only if you apply what you learn to your life

> James 1:21-25 – *Therefore, lay aside all filthiness and overflow of wickedness, and receive with meekness the implanted word, which is able to save your souls. But be doers of the word, and not hearers only, deceiving yourselves. For if anyone is a hearer of the word and not a doer, he is like a man observing his natural face in a mirror; for he observes himself, goes away, and immediately forgets what kind of man he was. But he who looks into the perfect law of liberty and continues in it, and is not a forgetful hearer but a doer of the work, this one will be blessed in what he does.*

What does this passage say the Word is able to do?

> ☐ *To save your soul*

5. The Word will <u>transform</u> your life if you <u>apply</u> what you learn to your life. (James 1:21-25) What does this passage say about being a hearer of the Word only?

> ☐ *Like a man who observes his natural face (external self – not the heart), and immediately forgets what he has learned because he has not examined his own heart in light of the truth of the Word.*
>
> ☐ *He has not 'exercised' what he has learned by applying the Word.*

6. We are to be <u>doers</u> of the Word and not <u>hearers</u> only (James 1:21-25)

What does it mean to be a 'doer' of the Word?

> ☐ *To do the 'work' that it takes to transform your life to line it up with the will of God revealed in the Word*

The Enemy's Lies vs. God's Truth

FACILITATOR'S GUIDE

RESOURCES NEEDED FOR THIS CLASS

- Lesson #2 In-Class Discussion Fill in the Blank form (available in Workbook and in the ADDITIONAL CLASSROOM MATERIALS FOR INDIVIDUAL LESSONS Section of this Facilitator Guide)

God loves you. Did you hear me? God loves you. No matter what you have done in your life, no matter how bad you think you are, or how far you have strayed from God - He loves you. He loves you so much that He sent his only Son to die on a cross and take the punishment for your sins upon Himself so that you can be reconciled to God. John 3:16 says God so loved the world that He gave His only begotten Son that whoever believes in Him should not perish but have everlasting life. That is Great News! God not only loves you – He knows every tiny detail about you because He created you just the way you are.

There is an enemy in this world that is intent on separating us from God. Sin entered the world in the Garden of Eden – when Satan tempted Adam and Eve to rebel against God by doing the one thing that God instructed Adam not to do - and they failed the test. (Read Genesis 2 & 3). At that time, sin entered into the world, and as a result we were all born sinners (Romans 3:10; 3:23).

Satan has been trying to destroy you since you were born. The Bible says that your enemy, the devil, prowls around like a roaring lion seeking someone to destroy (1 Peter 5:8). He is also referred to as the thief who comes to steal, kill and destroy (John 10:10). All of the negative things people have said to you or about you over the years were messages from the one who did not want to see you reconciled to God. People who said you were not good enough, that you would never amount to anything, and that you don't belong - were used as instruments by Satan to discourage you and separate you from God's truth about you.

The Bible says, just like Jeremiah, you were known by God before He formed you in your mother's womb (Jeremiah 1:5). He has a plan and a purpose for your life. In order to walk in your destiny, you need to see yourself like God sees you; truly understand your worth and refuse to listen to the voice of the enemy of your soul from this day forward.

Let God begin to show you His truth about your worth this week. As you read and study His Word and allow Him to speak to your heart, jot down what He wants you to apply to your life so you can share these jewels with your classmates next week.

This Week's Memory Verse:

Psalm 139:23-24 (NKJV) *"Search me, O God, and know my heart; try me, and know my anxieties; and see if there is any wicked way in me, and lead me in the way everlasting."*

Break down the memory verse:

What does it 'look like' to allow God to 'search' you?

What do you think it means to ask God to 'know your heart'?

When the Bible speaks of the "heart" (Definition from Unger 's Bible Dictionary) - it means:

- *Innermost center of the natural condition of man*
- *Center of thought and conception*
- *Laboratory and origin of all that is good and evil in thoughts, words, and deeds*
- *Seat of conscience*
- *Receptacle of the love of God*

What do you want God to do for you when you ask Him to 'lead you in the way everlasting'?

Questions for Discussion

- What did you learn from Psalm 139 that you can apply to your life in a practical way?
- Which lesson this week did you find the most difficult to complete? Why?
- Did you learn something new about yourself when studying this passage of Scripture? What was it?

Note for Facilitator: Help each person to see themselves in light of God's truth, not the world's standard for masculinity or femininity or any other aspect of their lives. God looks at the heart, and He created each person as a unique individual. It is the world and the enemy of our soul that urges us to look at other people and compare ourselves with them.

Go over some of the Homework questions ask participants to share their answers.

Fill in the blank Exercise (Located behind this week's homework in the Workbook, and in the appendix to this Facilitator Guide). Or use your imagination as a facilitator to make each lesson interesting and engaging for the participants utilizing some of the ideas presented in the "How to Use This Facilitator Guide" section on page 9.

The Enemy Has Been Trying to Destroy You

1. Your adversary, the devil, walks about like a roaring lion seeking to devour (1 Peter 5:8).

   - Ask participants to share particular situations from their lives where they know that the enemy of their soul tried to destroy them – and how they survived the attack.

2. Our enemy is the accuser of the brethren, who stands before God day and night pointing out what we have done wrong (Rev 12:10).

   The enemy uses people in your life to say things to hurt you, to constantly point out your flaws and berate you. Sometimes, we do this to ourselves.

- Ask participants to share what words or phrases they have adopted to describe themselves – spoken by other people or themselves.
- What effect has this had on their life?

Read Luke 22: 31-34.
In this passage, Jesus prays for Simon Peter, knowing that he will deny him three times that night. When Jesus is taken away to be crucified and the enemy 'sifts him as wheat', Simon Peter instinctively protects his 'flesh' over following his heart.

3. The enemy desires to sift us as wheat, but Jesus prays for us that our faith may not fail (Luke 22:31).

Despite what you have gone through in life –what trials and tribulations you have encountered along the way, what other people have said to you or done to you, what lies you have believed about yourself – Jesus believes in you and He wants you to return to Him for your strength and your healing.

As part of drawing us to Him initially and as part of our spiritual growth and sanctification process, sometimes God allows trials and tribulations into our life.

The Facilitator should share a personal example from his/her own life.
Read Job 1:8-2:10.

How did Job respond to the trials and tribulations he was experiencing?

What does this say about Job's character?

Does it appear from this passage that God loved or hated Job?

God Loves You
The Bible tells us that God loves us.

4. Before God formed you in your mother's womb, He knew you, and He sanctified you (Jeremiah 1:5, and Psalm 139:13).

Just like Jeremiah, you were known by God before He formed you in your mother's womb.

He has a plan and a purpose for your life.

God allows both good and bad into your life.

5. All things work together for good to those who love God and are the called according to His purpose. For those He foreknew he also predestined to be conformed to the image of Jesus (Romans 8:28-29).

Everything you have experienced in your life so far, and everything you will experience on this earth has a purpose – nothing is by chance. Despite your mistakes along the way, and the things you wish you had never done, God will work these things together for your good because you are CALLED.

God has a call on your life – that is why you are here. He wants you to know Him and His transformational power for your life because He is conforming you into the image of His son Jesus Christ.

6. <u>God</u> knows the <u>thoughts</u> He thinks towards you, thoughts of <u>peace</u> and not <u>evil</u> – to give you a <u>future</u> and a <u>hope</u> (Jeremiah 29:11).

   In order to walk in your destiny, in complete deliverance and healing, you need to see yourself like God sees you. Truly understand your worth and refuse to listen to the voice of the enemy of your soul from this day forward.

7. You are to be <u>strengthened</u> with might through <u>His Spirit</u> in the inner man, that <u>Christ</u> may dwell in your heart through <u>faith</u>, being <u>rooted</u> and <u>grounded</u> in love you may be able to comprehend what is the <u>width</u> and <u>length</u> and <u>depth</u> and <u>height</u> – to <u>know</u> the love of <u>Christ</u> (Ephesians 3:16-19).

Freedom in Truth

FACILITATOR'S GUIDE

RESOURCES NEEDED FOR THIS CLASS

- Lesson #3 In-Class Discussion Fill in the Blank form (available in Workbook and in the ADDITIONAL CLASSROOM MATERIALS FOR INDIVIDUAL LESSONS Section of this Facilitator Guide)

Jesus forgives, rescues, sets free and heals when we bring our brokenness to him. The Bible says that when we confess our sins, He is faithful and just to forgive us of our sins and to cleanse us from all unrighteousness (1 John 1:9).

There are numerous instances in the Bible where people called out or reached out to Jesus in their brokenness and asked Him for help, and He never turned them away. (Matthew 9:27-29; Mark 1:40-41; Luke 8:43-48; Matthew 20:29-34; Matthew 14:22-31). There are also instances where Jesus initiated the contact with a hurting person and healed them (John 5:1-9; Luke 13:10-13; John 4:1-26, 28). Finally, there are instances where others assisted another person to get to Jesus for healing, or they came to Him for healing on behalf of someone else (Luke 5:17-26; John 4:46-54).

In addition to those who sought healing from Jesus, there were people (even religious leaders) who exposed other's sins for the sake of public humiliation, as well as trying to trap Jesus in His response so they could justify killing Him (John 8:1-11). Other times, they did not physically expose the sinner but harbored ill will towards them in their hearts, and Jesus consistently responded to the sinner with mercy, grace, and forgiveness (Luke 7:36-50). The Bible also reveals that some people are afflicted with infirmities, not because of sin in their lives, but because God desires to use their lives and their testimony to reveal His glory. The story of the man who was blind from birth is one such example (John 9:1-11).

When others condemn you for what they see in your life, or you condemn yourself for your behavior, know that God is standing by to forgive you and cleanse you from all unrighteousness. He is waiting for you to expose your shortcomings to the light, to confess your sins to Him and allow Him to set you free so he can begin to heal your pain.

God's Word is truth, and if you abide in His Word, He will show you the truth about who He is, and how much He loves you. The truth He wants you to understand and incorporate into every aspect of your being will transform your life forever!

This Week's Memory Verse

John 8:31-32 (NKJV) *Then Jesus said to those Jews who believed Him, "If you <u>abide</u> in My word, you are My <u>disciples</u> indeed. And you shall <u>know</u> the truth, and the truth shall <u>make</u> you free."*

Break Down the Memory Verse:

Abide – in the King James Version it says to 'continue' in My Word - (to remain, not to depart, abide)

Disciple *(Definition from Unger 's Bible Dictionary)* – What does this mean? In the Greek language, mathetes = learner. Applies to one who professes to have learned certain principles from another and maintains them on the other's authority.

Know the truth (knowledge, perceive)

Make you free – set at liberty from the dominion of sin

Questions for Discussion:

- What 'little things' did God reveal to you in His Word this week that he wants you to apply to your life and you wrote down to share?
- Ask for volunteers to share instances when sin in their life was exposed by someone else
  - □ When was it exposed?
  - □ How was it exposed?
  - □ To whom was it exposed?
  - □ How did you feel?
  - □ What happened after exposure?

Go over some of the Homework questions and ask participants to share their answers.

Fill in the blank Exercise (Located behind this week's homework in the Workbook, and in the appendix to this Facilitator Guide). Or use your imagination as a facilitator to make each lesson interesting and engaging for the participants utilizing some of the ideas presented in the "How to Use This Facilitator Guide" section on page 9.

Jesus is merciful towards the sinner

Read John 8:1-11 (Woman Caught in Adultery)

- □ How do you think this woman felt as she was publicly exposed for her sin?
- □ What do you think she was thinking when Jesus stooped down and wrote on the ground with His finger? (verse 6)
- □ What do you think she thought about what He said to them when they continued asking Him about stoning her? (verse 7)
- □ How do you think she felt when they began to go away one by one? (verse 9)
- □ Do you think she was afraid when Jesus finally spoke to her? (verse 10-11)
- □ Did Jesus let her off the hook completely? (verse 11). No, He told her to go and sin no more.

1. Jesus does not condemn sinners, He forgives them. (John 8:1-11)

2. When we encounter Jesus and our <u>sins</u> are exposed to Him – he <u>forgives</u> our <u>sins</u> and tells us to go and <u>sin no more</u>. (John 8:11)

3. If we <u>confess</u> our <u>sins</u>, He is faithful and just to <u>forgive</u> us our <u>sins</u> and <u>cleanse</u> us from all <u>unrighteousness</u>. (1 John 1:9)

   Read Luke 7:36-50 (Woman Anoints Jesus' Feet)
   - How did the Pharisee react to the woman's actions *in his heart*? (verse 39)
   - How did Jesus respond to the Pharisee's judgmental heart? (verses 40- 47)
   - How did Jesus react to the woman? (verse 44)
   - What did Jesus say to her? (verses 48, 50)

4. Jesus reacts to our <u>repentance</u> with <u>forgiveness</u> and <u>mercy</u>. (Luke 7:44-50)

   - *Repent – means to change one's mind and turn from sin*

5. <u>Faith</u> in Jesus is what saves us and gives us <u>peace</u>. (Luke 7:50)

   What did these two women have in common?
   - *Both were sinners in need of grace*
   - *Both judged by other people for their conduct*
   - *Both came to recognize that Jesus is the one who saves*
   - *Both were treated by Jesus with dignity and grace – forgiven and set free*

   Jesus says something powerful to the judgmental Pharisee in this encounter with the woman. He asks the Pharisee a question through the parable of the two debtors (verses 41-43) – to which the Pharisee responds that the one who owes the most will love the one forgiving the debt more than the one forgiven little.

   He then turns to the woman to show the application to her life – that her sins are many (verse 47) and therefore, once she recognizes that He is the one who forgives and sets free from the bondage of sin, she loves Him much more than a person who has sinned little and is forgiven little.

Application

How does this apply to your life? Do you feel that the things that you have participated in – both in secret and openly – whether you acted on sinful desires, or just pondered it in your heart - puts you in the category of (sinning much)?

This passage of Scripture gives us hope. I believe that when we fall far short of the mark, and have strayed outside the will of God but we repented, sought forgiveness, and turned around as a result of recognizing who Jesus Christ is, we love Him deeper and with more passion than a person who has never fallen so far away.

This woman put aside her pride, humbled herself and fully exposed herself in front of this self-righteous religious leader. She came right up into His house and didn't worry about what Simon thought about her because she was seeking Jesus. She focused entirely on Jesus, and her love for Him – the only one who could save her and set her free from her sin.

As a result, Jesus publicly recognized this woman, using her as an example of a person who loves Him more than others and forgave her and gave her His peace. That is great news for you and me!

Begin to Share Testimonies

This is a preliminary exercise to allow the participants to get to know one another better by opening up and sharing about their lives. Keep to the time limit so each person gets a turn at sharing. This first exercise is not intended to get too 'deep' into their testimony.

Ask each participant to share 5 – 10 minutes (depending on time remaining)

- ☐ When did you first experience a life-controlling issue that you are not proud of (how old were you)?
- ☐ What do you think is the cause of your behavior?

Close Out with Prayer – Thank the participants for sharing and pray for them as they begin to expose their pain.

Hearing God's Voice

LESSON #4

FACILITATOR'S GUIDE

RESOURCES NEEDED FOR THIS CLASS

- Puzzle for Lesson #4: Make copies of Part 1, 2, and 3 of the Puzzle for each participant (available in the ADDITIONAL CLASSROOM MATERIALS FOR INDIVIDUAL LESSONS Section of this Facilitator Guide)
- Lesson #4 In-Class Discussion Fill in the Blank form (available in Workbook and in the ADDITIONAL CLASSROOM MATERIALS FOR INDIVIDUAL LESSONS Section of this Facilitator Guide)

God first spoke to man shortly after He created the first human beings. (Genesis 1:26-28). All throughout the Bible, we see instances where God spoke to people in various ways through:

- His Audible voice - Adam and Eve - Genesis 3; Samuel - 1 Samuel 3; Moses - Exodus 3; Abraham – Genesis 12; Elijah – 1 Kings 19:11-13; Gideon – Judges 6
- His Prophets – Samuel to Saul – 1 Samuel 15; Nathan to David – 2 Samuel 12; Jonah to the people of Nineveh – Jonah 3
- His Written Word – King Josiah – 2 Kings 22; People of Jerusalem - Nehemiah 8:1-11

When Jesus walked this earth in human form, He communicated directly with humanity through His teachings and interactions with people. In the book of John, Jesus reveals that He is the Good Shepherd and that His sheep know His voice (John 10:1-27). Jesus was saying, like sheep who know the voice of their shepherd (protector, provider, comforter), those who know Him as Lord and Savior know His voice.

As Jesus was nearing the end of His time on this earth, He promised that He would send the Holy Spirit to be with us and to speak to us after He departed this earth (John 14:25-26; John 16:12-15; Hebrews 10:15-16; 1 Corinthians 2:9-12). The Holy Spirit speaks to us today through promptings in our spirit.

God has been speaking to mankind in various ways ever since He created us, and the Bible tells us that He is the same yesterday, today, and forever (Hebrews 13:8). Therefore, we can be sure that He is speaking to you and me today. We just need to be still and learn to listen and know His voice.

When learning to hear the voice of God, keep in mind His character. God will never contradict His character when communicating with you. We know the character of God by studying His Word. You will know how God will react to circumstances and situations in your life by reading about how He has reacted to similar situations in the Bible.

This Week's Memory Verse

1 Corinthians 2:12 (NKJV) *Now we have received, not the spirit of the world, <u>but the Spirit who is from God</u>, that we might <u>know</u> the things that have been freely given to us by God.*

Break Down the Memory Verse:

- When we are born again, we have the deposit of God's Holy Spirit inside us
- Why have we received the <u>Spirit from God</u>?
- That we might <u>KNOW</u> the things that have been FREELY given to us by God
- What things do we know we have from God?
- The free gift of
  - □ *Salvation*
  - □ *Wisdom*
  - □ *Adoption*
  - □ *Eternal Life*
  - □ *The power to align our lives with God's Word*
  - □ *Freedom from the power of sin to rule us*

If we don't already **know** that we have freedom from the power of habitual sin it is like inheriting a fortune but you don't know that you have it.

Think for just a moment:

- What would your life look like today if you KNEW that you had access to the fortune left to you by someone in their will?
- What would your life look like today if you KNEW that you have the Power of the Holy Spirit living inside you to help you overcome all manner of sin that tries to grip you?
- What would your life look like tomorrow if you encountered a temptation that used to send you into the arms of another man or woman – but you now KNOW that you have the Power to walk away and live a life holy and pleasing to God every time temptation arises?
- You DO have the Power of God living inside you if you are a born-again Christian. You no longer have to give in to the desires of your flesh. God is right here helping you because you have HIS Spirit, not the spirit of the world.

Demonstration of the Lesson

To demonstrate the importance of receiving guidance from God for everything we do, we will use a practical hands-on demonstration.

Materials Needed: There is a SAMPLE PUZZLE is in back of Facilitator Guide – Lesson #4

- Puzzle or toy that requires following the instructions provided to be successful in solving the puzzle or completing the task (brain teaser, Lego construction kit, etc.)

Demonstration

- Divide the class into smaller groups.
- Give them the problem without any instructions (Lesson #4 – Part 1) of the puzzle and give them some time to wrestle with it.
- After 5 minutes of struggling with the problem, give them the instructions (Lesson #4 – Part 2) and a few more minutes to work on the problem.
- Finally, give them the solution (Lesson #4 – Solution).

Even if the problem is unsolvable in the few minutes the groups had to work on them, they likely found it better to have the instructions instead of being provided a problem with no information to solve it.

This exercise leads into the lesson for today.

God has given us His Word to guide and direct our lives. There is no human experience that cannot be informed by the living Word of God. Furthermore, God will guide and direct our steps every day as we learn to listen to His voice and obey His direction for our lives.

Go over some of the Homework questions and ask participants to share their answers.

Questions for Discussion:

What 'little things' did God reveal to you in His Word this week that He wants you to apply to your life and you wrote down to share?

Find out if any of the participants accepted Jesus Christ as their personal Lord and Savior for the first time as a result of the homework this week (Day 1 Question 4). If so, celebrate them and encourage them!

Ask participants to share how they have personally experienced God 'speaking' to them. How did they know it was God and how did they respond?

We learn to recognize the voice of God as we develop a personal relationship with Him. Just like developing a relationship with your friends, you have to work at developing your relationship with God. When you know someone very well, you can recognize their voice right away when they call you on the phone without even looking at the caller ID. The same is true with God. As you spend time with Him in prayer, worship, and the reading and studying of His word, you will begin to recognize His voice right away when He speaks to you.

As we learn to recognize the voice of God (over our own voice or the voice of the enemy), we can more readily respond to God's direction for our lives.

Fill in the blank Exercise (Located behind this week's homework in the Workbook, and in the appendix to this Facilitator Guide). Or use your imagination as a facilitator to make each lesson interesting and engaging for the participants utilizing some of the ideas presented in the "How to Use This Facilitator Guide" section on page 9.

God 'speaks' to His children in a variety of ways

Read Romans 1:19-20.

¹⁹because what may be known of God is manifest in them, for God has shown it to them. ²⁰For since the creation of the world His invisible attributes are clearly seen, being understood by the things that are made, even His eternal power and Godhead, so that they are without excuse,

1. God speaks to us through nature. (Romans 1:19-20)

   God has revealed His character (His attributes) to man clearly through the things that He created. What He is revealing in this passage is that there is no excuse for man to not know God and understand His attributes, for every person has experienced Him through nature. To witness the magnificence of a sunrise or sunset; to look at the intricacies of nature in plants, animals, humans; to know the faithfulness of God through the repetitive cycles of the day, week, month, year, and changing of the seasons; to look into the sky on a clear night and see the millions of stars and understand the vastness and complexity of space.

2. God speaks to us through the preached word. (Romans 10:14; 1 Corinthians 1:21; Acts 10:42).

3. God speaks to us through signs and wonders. (Exodus 4:1-9; Acts 4:22; Acts 5:12; Hebrews 2:1-4).

4. God speaks to us when we worship Him. (John 4:24; James 4:6; Acts 17:24-25).

5. God speaks to us through circumstances. (Acts 16:16-34).

   Nothing we experience in life is by 'accident' or by 'chance'. Sometimes, God speaks to us through circumstances. In reflection about that circumstance, you understand volumes about God's character and His will for your life and the lives of the people in your world.

   In Acts 16:16-34, Paul and Silas are in prison for commanding a demonic spirit to come out of a slave girl. While in prison, they were praying and singing hymns to the Lord when an earthquake shook the prison, breaking open all of the cells and loosing all of the prisoner's chains. The guard was so fearful that he would lose his life over the release of the prisoners that he determined to kill himself. Paul stopped him by letting him know that the prisoners were all still there. The guard fell trembling before Paul and Silas to ask how he and his household could be saved. That night the guard and his whole household were saved and baptized.

   God spoke to that guard through the circumstances he found himself in. It changed his life and the lives of his family members forever!

6. God speaks to us through His Word. (2 Tim 3:16; James 1:21-25).

   Close Out with Prayer – Thank the participants for sharing about how they have heard from God and their response to that voice.

Prayer – Communicating with God

LESSON #5

FACILITATOR'S GUIDE

RESOURCES NEEDED FOR THIS CLASS

- Lesson #5 In-Class Discussion Fill in the Blank form (available in Workbook and in the ADDITIONAL CLASSROOM MATERIALS FOR INDIVIDUAL LESSONS Section of this Facilitator Guide)

Prayer is one of the ways we communicate with God. We have already studied how God communicates with us. Now, we will focus on one of the ways we can communicate with God. As hard as it may be to comprehend, God really wants to hear from you. In fact, the Bible says that we are to pray without ceasing (1 Thessalonians 5:17). By this, we are to always be in a posture of prayer – talking to God and listening to Him.

There are no special requirements for prayer. Some people are unsure and even fearful about prayer because they have never been taught how to pray, or they have not spent time with others who are comfortable with prayer to learn from them. Some people think that God requires a special formula or eloquent words to be spoken before He will listen and respond. Nothing could be farther from the truth! If you don't believe me, let's look at some prayers in the Bible that were not lengthy or eloquent and were still answered by God:

- "Lord, save me!" (Matthew 14:30)
- "Now Hannah spoke in her heart; only her lips moved, but her voice was not heard..." (1 Samuel 1:13)
- "Jesus, Son of David, have mercy on me!" (Luke 18:38)
- "Therefore, give to Your servant an understanding heart to judge Your people, that I may discern between good and evil. For who is able to judge this great people of Yours?" (1 Kings 3:9)

God wants to hear from you. Prayer is a means to develop an intimate relationship with Him. Just like you spend time talking to your friends about everything in your life, talking to God about those same things is prayer. The Bible tells us that if we develop intimacy with Him and know His Word, our wills becomes aligned with the will of God and we can ask for whatever we want and it will be given to us (John 15:7).

Even when we don't know what to pray for or how to pray, God has already given every born-again Christian His Holy Spirit who makes intercession for us in accordance with the will of God (Romans 8:26-27). That is great news! God even gives us what we need to communicate with Him in prayer. If you don't already have a regular prayer life, begin right now and your life will never be the same!

This Week's Memory Verse:

1 John 5:14-15 (NKJV) [14]*Now this is the <u>confidence</u> that we have in Him, that if we ask anything <u>according to His will</u>, He hears us.* [15]*And if we know that He hears us, whatever we ask, we know that we have the petitions that we have asked of Him.*

Break Down the Memory Verse

- ☐ What is the <u>confidence</u> that we have in Him?
- ☐ How do we know that we are praying in <u>accordance with His will</u>?

God tells us in His Word that He will answer our prayers if we pray in accordance with His will. (See also John 14:13-14.)

Questions for Discussion:

What did God reveal to you in His Word about prayer this week that He wants you to apply to your life and you wrote down to share?

Ask if each participant has a prayer partner that they regularly pray with. If not, request that they partner with at least one other person in prayer for the remainder of the sessions. Explain the importance of praying with a prayer partner.

Go over some of the homework questions and ask participants to share their answers.

Fill in the blank Exercise (Located behind this week's homework in the Workbook, and in the appendix to this Facilitator Guide). Or use your imagination as a facilitator to make each lesson interesting and engaging for the participants utilizing some of the ideas presented in the "How to Use This Facilitator Guide" section on page 9.

Our Prayers Move God on our Behalf

1. God will <u>incline</u> His <u>ear</u> towards us when we pray (Psalm 116:2; Psalm 17:6; Psalm 10:17; 1 Peter 3:12).

2. God will sometimes <u>answer</u> our prayers before we <u>finish praying</u> (Isaiah 65:24).

3. God <u>hears</u> the prayers of the <u>afflicted</u> (Psalm 22:24; Jonah 2:2,7).

4. When we <u>humble</u> ourselves, and <u>pray</u>, and <u>turn</u> from our <u>wicked</u> ways, God will <u>hear</u> us. (2 Chronicles 7:14).

Power of Praying Scripture Back to God

Read Isaiah 55:11 *"So shall My word be that goes forth from My mouth; It shall not return to Me void, But it shall accomplish what I please, And it shall prosper in the thing for which I sent it."*

There is power in praying Scripture back to God. God honors His Word and it never returns to him void, meaning that what He purposed for His Word will come to pass (Isaiah 55:11).

Read Nehemiah 1:5-11. We also see God responding to Nehemiah's prayer because he is praying Scripture back to God.

In verse 9, Nehemiah reminds God of what was He promised in Deuteronomy 30:2-5, *"but if you return to Me, and keep My commandments and do them, though some of you were cast out to the farthest part of the heavens, yet I will gather them from there, and bring them to the place which I have chosen as a dwelling for My name."*

5. You can be <u>confident</u> that God will <u>do</u> what He has said in His <u>Word</u> (Isaiah 55:11).

6. When God has <u>promised</u> something specific in Scripture we can be <u>confident</u> that <u>God</u> will answer that prayer (Deuteronomy 30:2-5/Nehemiah 1:9).

Jesus Intercedes (Prays) on our Behalf

In addition to our praying to God for our needs to be met, we have a High Priest who intercedes on our behalf day and night. Jesus is our High Priest, and He uniquely understands our needs and frailties because He experienced life on this earth in human form. He now sits at the right hand of the Father in heaven and intercedes on our behalf. Even before He left this earth, Jesus began to pray for us.

Read John 17:6-26.
In this passage, Jesus is praying for His disciples just before He would be taken away and crucified. Notice how he prays. He specifically says in verse 9 that He doesn't pray for the world but specifically for those who are His disciples:

- He prays for unity in the body of believers (verse 11)
- He prays that they will be filled with His joy (verse 13)
- He prays that they will be sanctified with God's truth – His word (verse 17)

He then prays for all believers –that includes you and me – beginning in verse 20. He prays:

- That we would be unified so the world will know we are believers (verse 20)
- That we will be with Him in heaven (verse 24)
- That we will have His love (verse 26)

7. Jesus <u>prays</u> for <u>all</u> believers to be <u>unified</u> with Him (John 17:20-26).

8. Jesus <u>intercedes</u> on our behalf as our <u>High Priest</u> (Hebrews 7:25; 1 John 2:1).

9. <u>Jesus</u> is at the <u>right hand</u> of the Father <u>interceding</u> on our behalf (Romans 8:34).

Explain how participants are to complete the Timeline/Root Cause Exercise as part of the homework for Lesson #6. Go over the instructions in detail and ask if there are any questions about how to complete the exercise. This exercise is located after Lesson #6 Day 5 Homework of the Workbook. Participants should be encouraged to make a copy of this exercise before beginning to complete it, as it will continually be updated over the next several weeks.

TIMELINE/ROOT CAUSE EXERCISE

Instructions: This exercise is for your eyes only. It will not be turned in to the facilitators. However, we will discuss the results of the exercise in class, and recommend that you share what you are learning about yourself with your Accountability Partner. Write what you feel comfortable writing – to help you remember for processing and discussion later.

You will be creating a timeline of your life from birth to now as if you were preparing to write your autobiography. The purpose of this exercise is to help you:

- Identify the significant things/events that have occurred in your lifetime (good and bad, joyful and painful) that cause you to think and behave the way you do;
- Recognize patterns of behavior in your life; and
- See how it all fits together to make you the person you have become (warts and all).

Add to your timeline as God continues to reveal things to you over the next several weeks.

Instructions for Completion

1. Pray and ask God to help you complete this exercise.
2. Work through each of the statements below and write down anything that comes to your mind.
3. Create a timeline of your life from your earliest memories and make notes along your timeline so you can see how some things that have occurred in your life may have contributed to life-controlling issues, as well as patterns of behavior that you may not have been aware of before completing this exercise. Put your age next to significant milestones.
4. Write down what feelings you experienced at each major milestone on the timeline.
5. Pray and ask God to begin healing your heart for those past pains/disappointments.
6. Share some of what you are discovering about your life history and patterns with your Accountability Partner so they can pray for you more specifically.

Some Possible Root Causes of my life-controlling issues

1. Notes about my relationship with my mother and other significant women in my life from childhood until now.
2. Notes about my relationship with my father and other significant men in my life from childhood until now.
3. Significant things that happened to me over my lifetime (both good and bad). Note your age at each milestone.
4. How I have felt about myself from childhood until now.
5. My history of drug/alcohol use (earliest exposure, and most recent).
6. Anything else God is revealing to me about my life.

Timeline

For this exercise, you will use the next page to construct your own timeline.

(Note this example is from the author's life and will likely be very different from your experiences)

Example

Never felt like the sex God made me even in elementary school – did not fit in with the other boys/girls	Parents Divorced developed anger towards mother/father – disconnected	Started college – met new gay friends – felt connected to the group	First physical relationship with a person of same sex	Accepted Jesus as personal Lord and Savior	

Self-Conscious about body

1993   1996   2001   2003   2004   2006

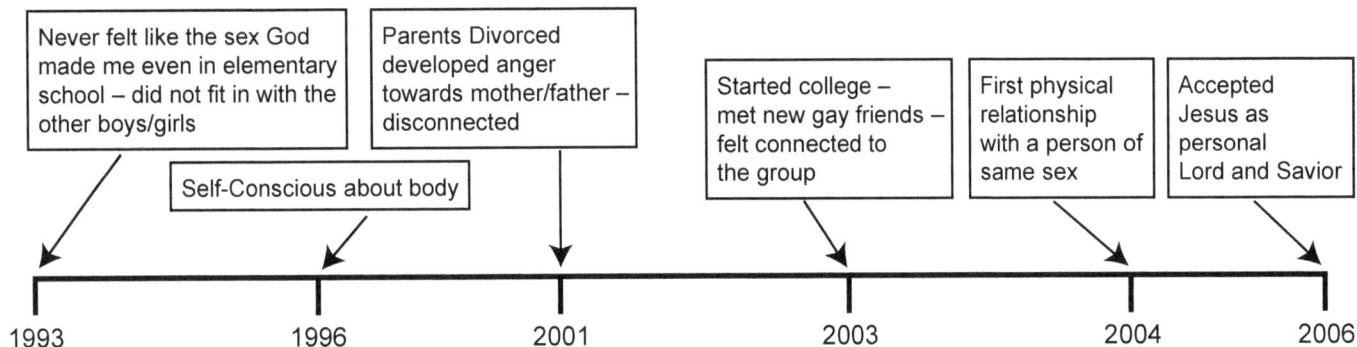

Feelings (example for a girl)

1993	*I never felt connected to other girls when I was young; I hung out with the boys and only played with them*
1996	*The kids in school made fun of me because I had a flat chest and didn't develop like the other girls. I felt embarrassed and ashamed about my body.*
2001	*When my parents divorced, I hated my mother because I felt that she didn't try to stay with dad. She wasn't there for me and I decided I didn't want to be like her.*
2003	*I met new friends in college that were gay; they were nice to me and accepted me for who I was. I finally felt like I belonged.*
2004	*My first sexual relationship with a woman was exhilarating. I felt like she really loved me and accepted me for who I am.*
2006	*Confused – want to line my life up with the Word of God but don't know how.*

Note – participants may wish to be creative in displaying the results of their timeline/root cause exercise. They may want to make a Vision Board to display where they have been and where they desire to go in the future with their life. You can find examples on the Internet to display in class

Close Out with Prayer – Thank the participants for sharing their experiences with prayer and encourage them to continue and to seek partnership with another person as a prayer partner, if they don't already have one.

Fall of Man Root Causes of Sin

LESSON #6

FACILITATOR'S GUIDE

RESOURCES NEEDED FOR THIS CLASS

- Lesson #6 In-Class Discussion Fill in the Blank form and Timeline/Root Cause Exercise (available in Workbook and in the ADDITIONAL CLASSROOM MATERIALS FOR INDIVIDUAL LESSONS Section of this Facilitator Guide)

Many of us have heard and know the story of Adam and Eve in the Garden of Eden where the serpent (devil) tempted them to eat of the tree of the knowledge of good and evil, which God specifically prohibited them from eating (Genesis 2:1-17; 3:1-6). At that moment, sin entered into the world and has been passed down through all generations of man (Romans 3:10; 3:23). As a result of their sin, and to keep them from eating of the tree of life and remaining in sin forever, God banished Adam and Eve from the Garden (Genesis 3:22-24).

The remainder of the Bible is about God's marvelous plan for reconciling us to Himself through the sacrificial love of Jesus Christ, who died on the cross for our sins so we could be restored to God through justification and the free gift of righteousness (Rom 5:16-19). In the end, when all is said and done, all people who have accepted Jesus Christ as Lord and Savior and begin allowing God to transform their lives so they can live holy and pleasing to God, will be saved and will have access to the tree of life as God makes all things new (Romans 10:9; 10:23; Revelation 21:1-8; 22:1-5).

You and I were born into sin. So were our parents, our grandparents, our brothers and sisters, our teachers, our

coaches, our pastors, our _____ – you name it, we were all born into sin. As you well know from your own life, sinners have a natural propensity to remain in the flesh and to sin. Therefore, people get hurt as a result of these sinful interactions with each other. Sometimes, people hurt other people on purpose, and at other times, it is not done with any kind of intent – it just happens.

This week, you will be working on your personal timeline (Timeline/Root Cause Exercise follows Week 6 Day 5 Homework in the Workbook) to begin to understand how the things that you have experienced over your lifetime, and your response to those things, has resulted in your life-controlling sin issues. Please be diligent about working on that exercise this week, as it will begin your healing process.

It is also vitally important that we remain (abide) in the Word of God every day (John 8:31-32) because that is how God reveals His truth to us and how He sets us free. Therefore, we will continue to have daily reading assignments for this week, but there will not be as many questions to answer so you can focus on your timeline.

This Week's Memory Verse

Romans 6:12 (NKJV) [12]*Therefore, do not let sin <u>reign</u> in your mortal body, that you should obey it in its <u>lusts</u>.*

Break Down the Memory Verse

- ☐ What does it mean to let sin <u>reign</u> in your body?
- ☐ What does it mean to obey your body in its <u>lusts</u>?

Questions for Discussion

As you studied Romans 5:12-6:14 this week, what did you learn that you can apply to your life?

Do you see how we no longer have to give in to the lusts of our flesh since Jesus died and took our sins to the grave with him?

What verses tell us that? *(Romans 6:2-7, 11)*

That is fantastic news! We just have to grab ahold of that truth and put it in to action when we are tempted.

You cannot allow the root causes of sin in your life to be an excuse to continue sinful behavior. True repentance of sin requires a turning-away from sin, which begins the restoration process.

Read Romans 6:12-14. What is this passage saying to you? Ask participants to share.

- ☐ *We don't have to go through life blindly following the lusts of our flesh as if we have no power or authority over our bodies.*
- ☐ *We are children of the most High God and we have the Power of the Holy Spirit working in and through our lives.*
- ☐ *We must present ourselves as alive – to God – because Jesus died on the cross to break the power of sin in our lives.*

When sin entered into the world in the Garden of Eden, as a result of the sin of Adam and Eve, it never left the world. It was passed down through every generation to be born including our grandparent's generation, our parent's generation and our own generation.

Have you ever heard the saying "hurting people hurt people"? That is a direct result of sin. Let's look at some examples of this from the Bible:

Abandonment

Read Genesis 21:8-16.

After Sarah and Abraham had a feast for Abraham's second son Isaac – the son promised by God - Sarah demanded that Abraham cast out her maid Hagar and Abraham's oldest son Ishmael, who was born to him by Hagar so that there would be no competition for Isaac's inheritance.

In verse 15, we see that Hagar put her son under a shrub and left him alone. To Ishmael, it must have felt like abandonment.

Hagar had been abandoned – driven out by the only family she knew – and she, in turn, abandoned her son by leaving him alone.

In Hebrews 13:5, God says "I will never leave you nor forsake you." The truth is, God will never abandon you.

Lies/Deceit and Trickery

In Genesis Chapter 27, we read the story of Jacob deceiving his father Isaac who was very old. The Bible says his eyes were so dim he could not see. Jacob deceived his father into blessing him instead of his older brother Esau, by pretending to be Esau. In this way, Jacob stole the birthright from his older brother.

Later in Genesis Chapter 29, Jacob falls in love with a woman named Rachel and desires to marry her. He goes to her father to ask for her hand in marriage, whereby he agrees to work for her father for seven years in order to marry her. After seven years of work, Rachael's father deceived Jacob. Leah, Rachel's older sister, was given to Jacob on his wedding night instead of Rachel.

Lies and deceit can trouble us for years. Whether we originate the lie or we believe the lie, it can easily affect the way we live our lives.

- Have you believed a lie about your sinful behavior?
- Did you buy into the worldview that it is just the way things are in this world?
- Did you think that God created you to rebel against him?

Satan wanted you to believe that lie about yourself and keep you in bondage to sin. In John 8:44, Jesus said regarding Satan "There is no truth in him. When he speaks a lie, he speaks from his own resources, for he is a liar and the father of it."

Sexual Abuse

2 Samuel Chapter 13 contains the story of Amnon, a son of King David, who had a beautiful half-sister named Tamar. Amnon was in love with his sister Tamar and was obsessing over her. He pretended to be ill and requested that Tamar come and take care of him. When she did, he grabbed her and raped her. After that the Bible says that that he hated her exceedingly. Tamar told her brother Absalom what happened to her, and later Absalom murdered Amnon.

Tamar had no reason to believe that she was in any kind of danger when she went to serve her brother Amnon. However, the sexual sin of her brother rocked her world and changed the course of her life forever.

Romans 8:28 says that all things work together for good to those who love God and are called according to His purpose.

Everything that has happened to us during our lives has combined to make us who we are today. God has a plan and a purpose for each of us – and we are being transformed into His image little by little as we experience the things of life (2 Corinthians 3:18).

- Can you begin to see how things that you have experienced in your life (both good and bad) have shaped you into the man or woman you have become?

We have to realize that our life on this earth is a testing ground where we are being prepared for eternity.

As born-again Christians (those who have surrendered their hearts to the Lordship of Jesus Christ), we need to understand that "we wrestle not against flesh and blood but against principalities and powers and the rulers of darkness of this age..." (Ephesians 6:12). Satan uses people and circumstances to try to keep us from loving and serving God.

As you have been working on your personal timeline this week, I suspect you have identified situations, circumstances, and people that have caused you to believe a lie about yourself, which led you to seek companionship with people who encourage you to live a life not pleasing to God, and drove a wedge between you and God.

Let's begin to expose the dark areas of our lives, so that the love of Christ can shed light with the truth and begin the healing process.

Sharing Timeline/Root Cause Exercise

Ask each participant to share what he/she discovered about their life while working on their timeline. Make sure to allow equal time for each one to share.

- Did you discover any root causes for your sin? Explain.

Close Out with Prayer – Thank the participants for sharing their timeline exercises with each other and encourage them to continue working on it and refining it as God reveals more and more to them.

Forgiveness

FACILITATOR'S GUIDE

RESOURCES NEEDED FOR THIS CLASS

- Lesson #7 In-Class Discussion Fill in the Blank form (available in Workbook and in the ADDITIONAL CLASSROOM MATERIALS FOR INDIVIDUAL LESSONS Section of this Facilitator Guide)
- Instrumental Music
- Extra Kleenex
- Different Room Set-up
- Ministry Evaluation Forms for completion during break next week (located in FORMS section of Facilitator Guide)

Forgiveness is a gift we want from God when we sin against Him, but not one that we can easily give to people who hurt us. Most people find it very difficult to forgive someone who has hurt them, and they hold on to that hurt – going over and over it in their minds, sometimes for years. That hurt and pain becomes like a cancer inside. After reliving the incident which caused the pain for a period of time, they bury it deep inside and it festers below the surface causing damage to their physical health and well-being, not to mention their relationships with others. There are studies that suggest that holding on to un-forgiveness affects the immune system and can lead to chronic pain, heart disease, cancer, and other ailments.

God places a high value on forgiveness, an incredibly high value, demonstrated by the fact that he sent His Son Jesus to die on the cross for the forgiveness of your sins and mine. The Bible says, "for if you forgive men their trespasses, your heavenly Father will also forgive you. But if you do not forgive men their trespasses, neither will your Father forgive your trespasses." (Matthew 6:14-15).

God also gives us a timeframe in which to forgive when someone has hurt us. The Bible says, "Be angry, and do not sin: do not let the sun go down on your wrath, nor give place to the devil."(Ephesians 4:26-27). We are to forgive the trespasses of our offenders before the end of the day. Paul spoke to the Corinthians regarding forgiveness as follows, "now whom you forgive anything, I also forgive. For if indeed I have forgiven anything, I have forgiven that one for your sakes in the presence of Christ, lest Satan should take advantage of us; for we are not ignorant of his devices." (2 Corinthians 2:10-11). Don't you know that Satan loves unforgiveness? What better way to keep Christians in bondage to pain and suffering. What better way to keep us from forgiving those who have hurt us and prevent restoration of our relationships with one another?

Bishop T.D. Jakes says, "Forgiveness is a gift you give yourself," and he is right about that! Oftentimes, we hold on to unforgiveness for so long that the person who has hurt us has moved on with their lives, oblivious to the pain that we are still holding on to as a result of something they did, said, or failed to do or say. The unforgiveness hurts only the one who is holding on to it.

This week as you continue to work on your Timeline/Root Cause Exercise (Lesson #6), identify people who have hurt you in the past that you have never forgiven. As you work through the exercises this week, release your unforgiveness to God and let Him begin to heal your wounds resulted from it.

This Week's Memory Verse:

Ephesians 4:31-32 (NKJV) [31]*Let all bitterness, wrath, anger, clamor, and evil speaking be put away from you, with all malice.* [32]*And be kind to one another, tenderhearted, forgiving one another, even as God in Christ forgave you.*

Some definitions of terms that may be unfamiliar:
- *Wrath – extreme anger*
- *Clamor – loud and confused noise or shouting*
- *Malice – intention or desire to do evil, or ill will*

Room Set-Up for the Forgiveness Exercise

- Dimmable lighting (or lamps)
- Soft instrumental background music
- Table set-up for semi-privacy
- Box of Kleenex for each table
- Put chairs in a circle for instructional lesson prior to the forgiveness exercise

Question for Discussion

What does our memory verse say about forgiveness?
- *We are to forgive others with the SAME forgiveness that Christ has extended to us. That means completely absolving the offender of the offense, as if it had never happened.*

The ONLY way we are able to forgive in this manner is to draw on the strength and love of Christ in us. In order to forgive, we first need to admit that we are unable to forgive on our own and we need to ask God to change our hearts. He WILL give you the grace to forgive.

Fill in the blank Exercise (Located behind this week's homework in the Workbook, and in the appendix to this Facilitator Guide). Or use your imagination as a facilitator to make each lesson interesting and engaging for the participants utilizing some of the ideas presented in the "How to Use This Facilitator Guide" section on page 9.

Lesson on Forgiveness – What Forgiveness is and What it is Not *(Adapted from Resolving Everyday Conflict, Ken Sande & Kevin Johnson, (Baker Books 2011) © Peacemaker Ministries).*

1. **Forgiveness is NOT Forgetting** (Isaiah 43:25) - Forgetting is passive (letting a memory fade over time). Forgiving is an ACTIVE process involving a conscious choice and a deliberate course of action.

   Read Isaiah 43:25. *"I, even I, am He who blots out your transgressions for My own sake; And I will not remember your sins."*

God is not saying here that He "can't" remember the sins. Rather, He WON'T remember them. He deliberately chooses NOT to remember our sins anymore after He has forgiven us.

Deciding NOT to remember the sin that someone has committed against you requires you to deliberately choose not to dwell on or recount that offense. This can take plenty of effort on our part.

Forgiveness is not a matter of whether we forget but rather how we choose to remember. When we choose not to dwell on an offense committed against us, God's grace covers us and those painful memories will begin to fade into the background.

2. **Forgiveness is NOT <u>Excusing</u>** (Psalm 32:5) - <u>Excusing</u> says "That's Ok", or "You couldn't help it", or implies in some way that "What you did wasn't really wrong".

    Forgiveness is the OPPOSITE of excusing. What forgiveness says is "We both know that what you did was wrong - it was without excuse - BUT since God has forgiven me, I forgive you.

    Read Psalm 32:5. *I acknowledged my sin to You, And my iniquity I have not hidden. I said, "I will confess my transgressions to the Lord," And You forgave the iniquity of my sin.* - Here David Acknowledges his sin and exposes it to the light knowing that God will forgive him.

    Forgiveness deals honestly with sin. The very fact that forgiveness is needed and granted indicates that what someone did was wrong and inexcusable.

What Forgiveness IS

3. **Forgiveness is a <u>radical decision</u>** (Romans 5:8) not to hold an offense against the offender. It means to release a person from punishment or penalty.

4. **Forgiveness is <u>undeserved</u> and <u>cannot</u> be <u>earned</u>** (Romans 5:8) - and it is very often an expensive decision.

    Read Romans 5:8. *But God demonstrates His own love toward us, in that while we were still sinners, Christ died for us.*

    While we were still sinners. Sin requires payment. There are consequences for sin. Our sin creates a debt that someone must pay. God, in His great mercy, planned a way for our debts to be paid through the death of Jesus Christ. Jesus paid the debt that we owed for our sins. He made the payment that we owed.

    What about when someone sins against you? That sin also creates a debt. That person owes you something. <u>NOW, you have a choice to make</u>: you can either TAKE payments on that debt or you can MAKE payments on that debt.

    Let me say that again: you can either TAKE payments on that debt or you can MAKE payments on that debt.

    <u>Taking</u> payments can be seen when you withhold forgiveness, dwell on the wrong, are cold and aloof towards the person who offended you, give up on the relationship, lash back, or plot revenge against them.

Making payments can be seen when you choose to pay the price for the other person's debt - releasing them from the penalty that they deserve to pay. This is exactly what Jesus did for you.

What does this look like in practice? Sometimes, God empowers you to do this in one easy payment: you decide to forgive and by God's grace, the debt is swiftly and fully canceled in your heart and mind.

Other times, when you have been deeply wronged, the debt may be too large to pay all at once. You may need to bear the impact of the other person's sin over a longer period of time.

You may have to fight against painful memories, speak gracious words when you want to lash out, you may even have to endure the consequences of an injury that the other person is unable or unwilling to repair. This is costly.

Just remember that you do not have what it takes in your own strength to forgive as Christ forgave you. You have to draw on what Christ has done for you. You have to draw on the grace of God which will enable you to forgive in this way.

5. **Forgiveness is an Expensive Decision.** Matthew 18:21-22 - *Then Peter came to Him and said, "Lord, how often shall my brother sin against me, and I forgive him? Up to seven times?" Jesus said to him, "I do not say to you, up to seven times, but up to seventy times seven.*

Here Peter asks Jesus how often do we have to forgive? What did Jesus say? He commands us to forgive exponentially. Not just one time but we are to forgive every time we are sinned against.

This is a hard teaching, isn't it??? If we truly want to live for Christ, we need to reflect his character in ourselves and in our interaction with other people.

There are Two Components of Forgiveness

6. **First, there is a Heart Component** or Vertical Component. (Romans 12:18)

The Heart component requires us to release the offense to God. It is an ATTITUDE of forgiveness. This is solely between you and God.

Romans 12:18 says *If it is possible, as much as depends on you, live peaceably with all men.* We are to maintain a loving and merciful attitude towards people who have offended us. This is an unconditional commitment that you make with God.

By His Grace alone, you choose not to dwell on the hurtful offense, or seek vengeance or retribution in thought, word, or action. Instead, you pray for that person and stand ready at any moment to forgive them if they are ready to repent and ask for your forgiveness.

We are commanded by God to maintain a readiness to forgive at all times. This is keeping our Hearts right before Him.

7. **The Second Component of Forgiveness** is the **Transactional** or **Relational** component. (Matthew 18:15)

The Horizontal component of forgiveness is between you and your offender.

Unless you are dealing with a minor sin that can be overlooked, GRANTING forgiveness and reconciling that relationship is conditional on the repentance of the other person.

Once they confess, you can extend forgiveness and release him from the offense, thereby restoring your relationship with them.

This step is NOT APPROPRIATE until the offender has acknowledged wrongdoing.

Matthew 18:15 states that you should try to reconcile with a person who has offended you. *"Moreover if your brother sins against you, go and tell him his fault between you and him alone. If he hears you, you have gained your brother."*

This is the beginning of several steps laid out in the Word about seeking reconciliation. BUT actual reconciliation requires the offending person to confess what they did that was wrong and seek forgiveness.

This may not happen. The offender may never acknowledge what they did was wrong and may never ask for forgiveness.

You are ONLY required to be willing to forgive and to TRY to reconcile with the offender. As far as it depends on you, you are to seek peace (Romans 12:18). Actual reconciliation requires both parties to do their part.

When we forgive as the Lord forgives us, we release an offender from the penalty of being separated from us, just like God removes that separation when He forgives us.

We don't hold wrongs against others. We don't think about the wrongs and we don't punish others for them. Forgiveness can be described as a decision to make 4 promises:

1. I will not dwell on this incident.

   This is a Heart Component between you and God. I won't let this incident be replayed over and over in my heart.

2. I will not bring this incident up and use it against you.

   This is a Relational Component between you and your offender.

3. I will not talk to others about this incident.

   This is a Relational Component between you and your offender. You promise not to continue to keep the offense alive by talking to others about it.

4. I will not allow this incident to stand between us or hinder our personal relationship.

   This is a Relational Component between you and your offender. You promise not to build a wall between you and that person that would hinder your personal relationship with them. This is tough.

You may be saying to yourself something like this: "My friend did something so terrible - I <u>can</u> forgive him/her if he/she asks for my forgiveness, but I just can't forget what he/she did and I don't know if we can continue to be friends." That is an empty form of forgiveness and does not meet the 4 promises of forgiveness.

How do you think you would feel if you sinned against God - you repented and sought his forgiveness - and He said, "I forgive you, but I can't ever be close to you again." Would you feel like God really forgave you?

Practical Exercise on Forgiveness *(requires at least 30 minutes to an hour)*

- Choose one person that you identified this week during your homework exercises that you have not yet forgiven for what they did or failed to do.
  - □ If a participant states that he/she has no unforgiveness towards others, ask them if they need to forgive themselves for things he/she has done or 'allowed' to happen, or if he/she has unforgiveness towards God for allowing the things he/she has experienced in his/her life.
- Write a letter to God expressing your "attitude of forgiveness", your willingness to forgive that person regardless of whether they have asked for forgiveness or not, or even if they have passed away and are no longer alive. Completely release that person from the offense(s) in your letter to God. Be specific. These letters will not be shared with anyone unless you choose to share them.
- After you express your complete forgiveness of that person, write a prayer of blessing over the life of the person who has offended you. Pray that God will bless them (Matthew 5:44).
- Pray and ask God to heal your heart from the pain of the offense.

Close Out with Prayer

Sexual Integrity

LESSON #8

FACILITATOR'S GUIDE

RESOURCES NEEDED FOR THIS CLASS

- Lesson #8 In-Class Discussion Fill in the Blank form (available in Workbook and in the ADDITIONAL CLASSROOM MATERIALS FOR INDIVIDUAL LESSONS Section of this Facilitator Guide)
- Copies of Sexual Purity Resolution (Located in the Workbook and in the FORMS section of this Facilitator Guide)

What is sexual integrity? The definition of *integrity* is steadfast adherence to a strict moral or ethical code, the quality or condition of being whole or undivided (The American Heritage Dictionary of the English Language, 3rd Edition). Therefore, sexual integrity requires that we maintain a steadfast adherence to a strict moral or ethical code (biblical laws and principles) with respect to our sexual conduct. We have learned from the Word of God that there is absolutely no sexual conduct that is authorized by God outside the confines of marriage between one man and one woman.

We live in a highly sexually-charged society. You can't watch television, listen to the radio, pick up a magazine, or surf the Internet without being constantly bombarded with sexually charged stimulus. That is because we live in a fallen world raging from the effects of sin. People of the world follow after the lusts of the flesh and perpetuate this addiction through all forms of media. But we are called to be set apart from the world. God's will for us is our sanctification: that we should abstain from sexual immorality and know how to possess our bodies in sanctification and honor, not in passion of lust, like those who do not know God (1 Thessalonians 4:3-5)

You may be thinking this is easier said than done! And you are absolutely right. It is not easy, but we also have a promise from God: no temptation has overtaken you except such as is common to man; but God is faithful, who will not allow you to be tempted beyond what you are able, but with the temptation He will also make the way of escape, that you may be able to bear it (1 Corinthians 10:13).

In addition to studying Scriptures to help us in the area of sexual purity, we will also learn about some practical things we can do to diminish the raging desires of our carnal bodies that have been opened up and exposed to sexual impurity, until those desires fade over time. They will fade and no longer have the power to control you! Likewise, you also reckon yourselves to be dead indeed to sin, but alive to God in Christ Jesus our Lord. Therefore, do not let sin reign in your mortal body, that you should obey it in its lusts. And do not present your members as instruments of unrighteousness to sin, but present yourselves to God as being alive from the dead, and your members as instruments of righteousness to God. For sin shall not have dominion over you, for you are not under law but under grace (Romans 6:11-14).

Even after we have removed the things that feed our sexual addictions, have disassociated ourselves from the people we used to sin sexually with, have stopped going to the places we used to go to that enabled us to sin, and we have done everything we know to do to put guards in place to protect us, we will still face temptations that will challenge us to revert back to our old habits. While you will not be protected from temptations that come your way, you must know that God will ALWAYS make a way of escape for you when you are faced with such temptations. 1 Corinthians 10:13 says, "No temptation has overtaken you except such as is common to man; but God is faithful, who will not allow you to be tempted beyond what you are able, but with the temptation will also make the way of escape, that you may be able to bear it." Isn't it incredible to know that God knows what you can bear? You may think that you are being tempted beyond what you can overcome, but God created you and knows you better than you know yourself. Look for the escape route that He has provided to you EVERY time you are tempted.

Furthermore, James 1:12 says, "Blessed is the man who endures temptation; for when he has been approved, he will receive the crown of life, which the Lord has promised to those who love Him." God encourages us to *endure* temptations when they arise. Endure means to bear with tolerance, or suffer patiently without yielding (The American Heritage Dictionary of the English Language). You CAN endure the temptations that come your way, and when you do, you will be rewarded. These temptations are temporary attempts by the enemy to get you to satisfy your flesh. When Satan is unsuccessful in his attempts to get you to revert back and dishonor God, he will leave. The word of God says, "Resist the devil and he will flee from you." (James 4:7) Resist the enemy of your soul and use the escape route that God has provided to you! Each time you endure the temptation and do not sin, you become stronger and stronger in the Lord.

This Week's Memory Verse:

1 Corinthians 6:18 (NKJV) *Flee sexual immorality. Every sin that a man does is outside the body, but he who commits sexual immorality sins against his own body.*

Break Down the Memory Verse

Why is it so important that we not <u>sin against our own bodies</u>?

- ☐ *Our Body is the Temple of the Holy Spirit* (1 Corinthians 6:19-20)
- ☐ *God bought us at a price, and placed a deposit of His Holy Spirit inside us – and we are not to grieve the Holy Spirit* (Ephesians 4:30)

Questions for Discussion

Did you find this week's homework difficult? Why or why not?

Did you reach out to your Accountability Partner this week? Are you keeping him/her informed of your prayer needs as you continue in this study?

Go over some of the homework questions and ask participants to share their answers.

Fill in the blank Exercise (Located behind this week's homework in the Workbook, and in the appendix to this Facilitator Guide)

Sexual Integrity and Sexual Impurity

It is important to note where temptation to sin originates.

1. <u>God</u> does not tempt us to sin; we are tempted by <u>evil</u> when we are <u>drawn</u> away by our own <u>desires</u> and enticed (James 1:13-14).

   James 1:13-14 - *¹³Let no one say when he is tempted, "I am tempted by God"; for God cannot be tempted by evil, nor does He Himself tempt anyone. ¹⁴But each one is tempted when he is drawn away by his own desires and enticed.*

   Our carnal bodies are programmed to sin as a result of the fall of man. We have inherited this sin-nature from our parents who inherited it from their parents who inherited it from their parents, and on it goes back to Adam and Eve in the Garden of Eden. God knows that we are sinners in need of a Savior and so he has already made provisions for us through the shed blood of Jesus Christ.

   He also helps us day by day by helping us overcome this propensity to sin. Let's look at 1 Corinthians 10:13.

2. <u>When</u>, not if we are <u>tempted</u> to sin, God will make a way of escape for us (1 Corinthians 10:13).

   1 Corinthians 10:13 - *No temptation has overtaken you except such as is common to man; but God is faithful, who will not allow you to be tempted beyond what you are able, but with the temptation will also make the way of escape, that you may be able to bear it.*

   Sexual sin begins with the eyes and the mind. Your mind is so powerful that it triggers a physical reaction in your body when you allow your eyes to gaze on a sexual stimulus, and you allow your mind to begin to fantasize sexually.

   Jesus said that we can sin sexually with our eyes and mind alone. Let's look at Matthew 5:27-28.

3. We sin against God <u>sexually</u>, when we look <u>lustfully</u> with our eyes at another person (Matthew 5:27-28).

   Matthew 5:27-28 - *²⁷"You have heard that it was said to those of old, 'You shall not commit adultery.' ²⁸But I say to you that whoever looks at a woman to lust for her has already committed adultery with her in his heart.*

   Long before Jesus walked the earth in human form, another man of God already recognized the power of the eyes and mind to bring sexual sin into one's life.

   The Bible tells us to flee sexual immorality because:

4. Every sin that a man does is outside the body, but he who commits <u>sexual immorality</u> sins against his own <u>body</u>. (1 Corinthians 6:18)

   This week on Day 3 of the Homework, we looked at triggers in our lives that can lead to compulsive sexual behaviors. We learned that H.A.L.T. is an acronym that stands for Hungry, Angry, Lonely, and Tired, which represents 'red flags' indicating that you are vulnerable to act out, and do something you will later regret. You were requested to write a proactive/preventative plan and reactive/curative plan to deal with your personal triggers related to HALT.

- Examples from Scripture
  - ☐ HUNGRY (Esau sold his birthright – Genesis 25:29-34)
  - ☐ TIRED (Elijah is discouraged after his encounter with the prophets of Baal – 1 Kings Chapters 18 & 19)
- Ask participants to share the results of their self-assessments.

If you don't get your 'triggers to acting out' under control, you are prone to continue falling into sexual sin. The Word of God tells us that we become slaves to sin when we commit sin. Sexual sin controls our lives.

5. Whoever <u>commits</u> sin is a <u>slave</u> to sin. (John 8:34)

   John 8:34 - *Jesus answered them, "Most assuredly, I say to you, whoever commits sin is a slave of sin.*

   In the book of Romans, Paul describes an inward war between his flesh and his soul. He says that even though he willed to do good, evil was always present in his carnal body. This is exactly what we face today, especially with respect to sexual sin that we have allowed to enter into our lives.

The Mind and the Heart

All sexual immorality begins with a thought. It involves a lustful thought in your mind. That is why it is so important not to allow your mind to dwell on lustful thoughts!

The Word of God tells us that we are to cast down arguments and every high thing that exalts itself against the knowledge of God, bringing every thought into captivity to the obedience of Christ.

6. Cast down arguments and every <u>high thing</u> that exalts itself against the knowledge of God, bringing every <u>thought</u> into <u>captivity</u> to the <u>obedience</u> of Christ. (2 Corinthians 10:5)

   2 Corinthians 10:5 - *casting down arguments and every high thing that exalts itself against the knowledge of God, bringing every thought into captivity to the obedience of Christ*

   When those sexually immoral thoughts come into your mind, Scripture says to cast them down – don't dwell on them – take those thoughts captive to the feet of Jesus, where He has washed away our sins, so we no longer have to be enslaved to sin.

7. To be <u>carnally</u> minded is <u>death</u>, but to be <u>spiritually</u> minded is <u>life</u> and peace (Romans 8:6).

   Romans 8:6 - [6]*For to be carnally minded is death, but to be spiritually minded is life and peace.*

   We have to train our minds and hearts to think about and dwell on spiritual things and not allow our minds and hearts to dwell on things of the flesh that bring death to our souls.

8. We must set our minds on things <u>above</u> not on things on the <u>earth</u> (Colossians 3:2).

Colossians 3:2 - *²Set your mind on things above, not on things on the earth.*

Scripture tells us that we must also guard our hearts because out of our heart, springs the issues of life, including sexual immorality. The best way to do this is to meditate on the Word of God. Fill your heart with the Word, so full that there is no room for immoral thoughts.

9. Guard your <u>heart</u> by <u>meditating</u> on the <u>Word</u> to protect yourself from sexual immorality. (Proverbs 4:23, Matthew 15:19, Psalm 119:11)

Proverbs 4:23 - *Keep your heart with all diligence, For out of it spring the issues of life.*

Matthew 15:19 - *For out of the heart proceed evil thoughts, murders, adulteries, fornications, thefts, false witness, blasphemies.*

Psalm 119:11 - *Your word I have hidden in my heart, That I might not sin against You.*

Final Thoughts

It is important to understand that as we are remembering and discussing our personal sexual sins, and thinking about them as we have been completing our homework assignments, the enemy of your soul has been waging a battle against you – bringing to your remembrance the momentary pleasures you experienced when you participated in these sexual sins.

Satan never reminds you of the after-effects of sin –the guilt and shame associated with it– when he is enticing you. You may find yourself being especially prone to slipping up and 'acting out' despite your best efforts to avoid this.

The enemy of our souls has been trying to destroy each one of us since we were born, and even before some of us were born. Scripture says, "Be sober, be vigilant; because your adversary the devil walks about like a roaring lion, seeking whom he may devour (1 Peter 4:8). Keep this in mind and be extra vigilant to the tricks of the enemy. Ask your Accountability Partner to cover you in prayer as you work through these assignments.

Also know that there is great news if you do slip up! Jesus sees your heart, and He knows that you are exposing these past sins in order to heal and be completely delivered. He will forgive you if you confess your sin and get right back on track.

10. If we <u>confess</u> our sins, His is faithful and just to <u>forgive</u> us our sins and to <u>cleanse</u> us from all unrighteousness. (1 John 1:9)

1 John 1:9 - *If we confess our sins, He is faithful and just to forgive us our sins and to cleanse us from all unrighteousness.*

Go over Sexual Purity Resolution and Encourage Participants to sign it (located after Lesson #8 Day 5 Homework in the Workbook, and in the Forms section of this Facilitator Guide).

Close Out with Prayer

Spiritual Warfare

LESSON #9

FACILITATOR'S GUIDE

RESOURCES NEEDED FOR THIS CLASS

- Lesson #9 In-Class Discussion Fill in the Blank form (available in Workbook and in the ADDITIONAL CLASSROOM MATERIALS FOR INDIVIDUAL LESSONS Section of this Facilitator Guide)

Spiritual warfare is something every true Christian faces. In fact, the Word of God says that we should not be surprised when fiery trials come into our lives, as though something strange were happening to us (1 Peter 4:12). When you accept Jesus Christ as Lord of your life, walk away from the things of the world, and turn your attention and your life towards the things of God, you become a target for the enemy who wants you back under his dominion and control.

The Bible tells us that we are to be self-controlled and alert because the devil prowls around like a roaring lion seeking someone to devour (1 Peter 5:8). We must understand how the enemy operates so he cannot take advantage of us (2 Corinthians 2:11). Thankfully, the Bible gives us instructions on how to identify the works of the enemy and how to arm ourselves for spiritual battle. This week, we will study the armor of God, which provides spiritual protection when we face spiritual warfare. We will also study the battle plans of the enemy so we will understand how he operates so we can defeat him.

This Week's Memory Verse

2 Corinthians 10:3-5 (NKJV) ³*For though we walk in the flesh, we do not war according to the flesh.* ⁴*For the weapons of our warfare are not carnal but mighty in God for* <u>*pulling down strongholds,*</u> ⁵*casting down arguments and every high thing that exalts itself against the knowledge of God, bringing every thought into captivity to the obedience of Christ,*

Break Down the Memory Verse

What does it mean to '<u>pull down strongholds</u>'?

- *Strongholds are fortresses – high, thick walls that in biblical times were built to protect cities from enemy attacks.*
- *Strongholds – in the case of spiritual warfare - are incorrect thinking patterns that are constructed in our lives by the enemy of our souls.*
  - ☐ *Strongholds are built on lies and deception.*
  - ☐ *These strongholds are very hard to tear down because any attempt to pull them down is met with great resistance as the enemy will work hard to rebuild and keep them in place.*

□ *Spiritual strongholds are torn down by replacing incorrect thinking patterns with the Truth – the Word of God.*

How do we tear down these strongholds? What does our Scripture say?

- *Cast Down (throw down) arguments and every high thing that exalts itself against the knowledge of God – that exalts itself against the TRUTH.*
- *How do we know the Truth?*
  □ *The Word of God is Truth*

What else do we have to do?

- *Bring every thought captive to the obedience of Christ.*
- *Tie up and bind up every thought that comes into your mind– bring it to Jesus and compare it with the Word of Truth – do they agree or disagree?*
- *Romans 12:2 - And do not be conformed to this world, but be transformed by the renewing of your mind, that you may prove what is that good and acceptable and perfect will of God.*

Go over some of the homework questions and ask participants to share their answers.

Belt of Truth – the Truth is the truth of God's Word. Notice that the belt is the central piece of armor that holds many of the other pieces of armor in place. How does this relate spiritually?

- It is a foundational piece of armor.
- The Truth of God's Word is the basis for our faith.
- The breastplate is fastened to it.

Breastplate of Righteousness – Righteousness refers to the 'right standing' we now have because of what Jesus did for us on Calvary, and has nothing to do with our own worthiness apart from Christ. What do you notice about the breastplate that applies to your life spiritually?

- It protects the heart and vital organs.
- It shields me from attacks on the core of who I am.
- I am secure in the knowledge that I am in right standing with God because of Jesus.

Shoes of the Preparation of the Gospel of Peace – The Gospel is the "Good News" that Jesus came to die for our sins, and that when we accept Him as Lord and Savior, our sins are wiped clean and we have everlasting life with Him. What do you notice about the soldier's shoes that you can apply to your life spiritually?

- Helps me to stand still and firm footing on the Rock
- I don't have to run – I am secure in Jesus – I am at peace

Shield of Faith – Faith is the substance of things hoped for and the evidence of things not seen (Hebrews 11:1). Pay particular attention to what the shield of faith does for you in verse 16. How does this piece of armor relate to your life spiritually?

- The shield of faith extinguishes all of the fiery darts of the enemy! It encapsulates them and snuffs them out!
- My faith in Jesus Christ is powerful! It is the first line of defense when I am attacked by the enemy.
- I must rely on Jesus to fight my battles for me.

Helmet of Salvation – Salvation brings wholeness and deliverance from your sinful past. Think about what the helmet protects in light of what we have been discussing over the past couple of weeks. What do you see about the helmet that protects you spiritually?

- It protects my mind from the lies of the enemy.
- I have the mind of Christ.
- The mind is the greatest battlefield. When my mind stays on Christ, I am at peace.

Sword of the Spirit – The Scripture says the Sword of the Spirit is the Word of God. What kind of weapon is a sword? Is it used for aggression or defense (or both)? How does this weapon apply to your life spiritually?

- The Word of God is so powerful that Jesus used it against the enemy when He was tempted by Satan in the wilderness.

- Hebrews 4:12 says, *"For the word of God is living and powerful, and sharper than any two-edged sword, piercing even to the division of soul and spirit, and of joints and marrow, and is a discerner of the thoughts and intents of the heart."*

Fill in the blank Exercise (Located behind this week's homework in the Workbook, and in the appendix to this Facilitator Guide). Or use your imagination as a facilitator to make each lesson interesting and engaging for the participants utilizing some of the ideas presented in the "How to Use This Facilitator Guide" section on page 9.

Primary weapons of the enemy – how he wages battle against us

1. **Deception** – the stronghold is an incorrect thinking pattern that stems from believing something that is not true

   - Adam and Eve – Genesis 3:4-5 – The devil told Eve she would not surely die if she ate of the fruit of the tree.
     - God's truth – God told Adam not to eat of the tree or he would surely die (Genesis 2:16).

2. **Temptation** – when we are enticed to sin – devil makes it 'look good'

   - Eve – The devil made Eve see that the tree was good for food and it was pleasant to the eyes and desirable to make one wise (lie from the enemy). She and Adam ate it (Genesis 3:6).
     - God's truth – The first sin resulted in spiritual death and separation between God and man.

3. **Accusation** – devil then condemns you for what he enticed you to do

   - Satan is called the accuser of the brethren (Revelation 12:10). He accuses us of sin before God day and night
   - He also plants seeds of doubt in our minds – anything to get us to stop believing God and trusting Him.

How are the weapons of the devil used to attack people caught up in life-controlling sinful behaviors, and how do we fight back?

1. **Deception** – I have experienced negative things in my life and therefore, I am not loved.

   a. **Belt of Truth** - Truth of God's Word – Jeremiah 31:3 – *"...I have loved you with an everlasting love; Therefore with lovingkindness I have drawn you."*

   b. **Sword of Spirit** - God's Word

      i. John 3:16 – *"For God so loved the world that He gave His only begotten Son, that whoever believes in Him should not perish but have everlasting life."*

      ii. Isaiah 43:18-19 – [18]*"Do not remember the former things, Nor consider the things of old. [19]Behold, I will do a new thing, Now it shall spring forth; Shall you not know it? I will even make a road in the wilderness And rivers in the desert."*

2. **Temptation** – to believe that whatever the enemy is dangling before me as an unholy temptation is what I need and want

    a.   Satan makes this look good but we know it is not God's will for our lives.

    b.   James 4:7 says, *"Therefore submit to God. Resist the devil and he will flee from you."* Submit to the truth of God's word and resist the temptations of the enemy of your soul.

3. **Accusation** – if you submit to the temptation and go where you have no business going, the devil then accuses you and condemns you for your sin.

    a.   **Shield of Faith** – use this weapon to extinguish the fiery darts of the enemy

    b.   **Repent** and ask Jesus for forgiveness – 1 John 1:9 says, *"If we confess our sins, He is faithful and just to forgive us our sins and to cleanse us from all unrighteousness."*

    c.   **Jesus does not condemn** - John 3:17 - *For God did not send His Son into the world to condemn the world, but that the world through Him might be saved.*

Do not be afraid of the attacks of the enemy.

You have the <u>authority</u> to cast out demons. (Luke 10:19)

Luke 10:19 - *"Behold, I give you the authority to trample on serpents and scorpions, and over all the power of the enemy, and nothing shall by any means hurt you."*

Close Out with Prayer

The Heart

FACILITATOR'S GUIDE

RESOURCES NEEDED FOR THIS CLASS

- Lesson #10 In-Class Discussion Fill in the Blank form (available in Workbook and in the ADDITIONAL CLASSROOM MATERIALS FOR INDIVIDUAL LESSONS Section of this Facilitator Guide)

When Scripture refers to the 'heart', it is usually not referring to the physical muscle in your chest that pumps blood throughout your body. According to the *New Unger's Bible Dictionary*, the word 'heart' in Scripture means a variety of things, including:

- The center of the bodily life, the reservoir of the entire life-power (Psalm 40:8, 10, 12)
- The center of the rational-spiritual nature of man (Esther 7:5, 1 Corinthians 7:37)
- The seat of love and hatred (1 Timothy 1:5, Leviticus 19:17)
- The center of the moral life from highest love of God to hardening of the heart (Psalm 73:26, Isaiah 6:10, Jeremiah 16:12)
- The laboratory and origin of all that is good and evil in thoughts, words, and deeds (Matthew 12:34, Mark 7:21)
- The rendezvous of evil lusts and passions (Romans 1:24)
- The seat of conscience (Hebrews 10:22, 1 John 3:19-21)

Many of the references above seem to be tied to <u>emotions</u>. Other references to the heart in Scripture reveal that it is also tied to the <u>mind</u> or intellect of a man, and it can understand (John 12:40, Ephesians 1:8). The heart is also tied to the <u>will</u> of man (Exodus 25:2, 35:5).

Additionally, the heart is closely connected with the 'soul' having, as one meaning, the seat of the feelings, desires, affections, and aversions of a man *(New Unger's Bible Dictionary)*. In other words, the heart is tied to the <u>conscience</u> of a man.

As you can see, the scriptural heart is very closely tied to the mind, will, emotions, and conscience of a person. God has said repeatedly in His Word that we are to love Him and serve Him with our whole heart (Deuteronomy 6:5, 11:13, 13:3, Joshua 22:5, Jeremiah 29:13, Matthew 22:37, Mark 12:30, Luke 10:27). In order to love and serve Him well, we must have our hearts right with God.

Proverbs 27:19 says, *"As in water face reflects face, so a man's heart reveals the man,"* Therefore, it is *extremely important that our hearts are pure and clean. Create in me a clean heart, O God, and renew a steadfast spirit within me.* (Psalm 51:10) We also must be very careful not to allow our hearts to become hard and incapable of receiving the love and affection of God (Ephesians 4:18, Proverbs 28:14).

If you have allowed your heart to become hard and calloused as a result of the things you have experienced in your life, there is great news! God is in the business of heart transplants and He says, *"I will give you a new heart and put a new spirit within you; I will take the heart of stone out of your flesh and give you a heart of flesh."* (Ezekiel 36:26)

This Week's Memory Verse:

Proverbs 4:23 (NKJV) *Keep your heart with all diligence, for out of it spring the issues of life.*

Break Down the Memory Verse

- Keep (Strong's number 5341) means – guard, watch, watch over, preserve
- Heart (Strong's number 3820) means inner man, mind, will, heart, understanding, soul, thinking, conscious
- Diligence (Strong's number 4929) means – place of confinement, prison, guard, jail, observance
- Issues (Strong's number 8444) means outgoing, border, a going out, source (of life)

Overall meaning of the passage: *Guard your inner man with all fortifications, for out of your heart springs the source of life.*

Discussion

Go over the homework assignment and ask participants to share their answers to some of the questions presented.

Fill in the blank Exercise (Located behind this week's homework in the Workbook, and in the appendix to this Facilitator Guide). Or use your imagination as a facilitator to make each lesson interesting and engaging for the participants utilizing some of the ideas presented in the "How to Use This Facilitator Guide" section on page 9.

1. We are cursed when we trust in people to give us strength and allow our hearts to depart from God (Jeremiah 17:5).

   Jeremiah 17:5 - *Thus says the Lord: "Cursed is the man who trusts in man And makes flesh his strength, Whose heart departs from the Lord.*

   When we enter into an unhealthy emotional relationships with other people, we turn him/her and our relationship with him/her into an idol. This is sin in eyes of God. His Word gives us instruction about what we are to do in this instance; similar to other types of sin we have studied over the past couple of weeks. Turn to 1 Corinthians 10:14. What does the Word say we are to do?

2. We are to flee from idolatry (1 Corinthians 10:14).

   1 Corinthians 10:14 - *Therefore, my beloved, flee from idolatry.*

<u>Engage the participants in conversation</u>: Ask for volunteers to answer the questions below. If no response is offered, the sub-bullets may provide enough to get the conversation started.

Where do you think the line is between 'friendship' and 'idolatry'?

- □ *When you become 'obsessed' with him/her*
- □ *When you feel like you can't live without him/her – talking to him/her and seeing him/her every day*
- □ *When you have absolutely no friends except for the one you are emotionally tied to*

If you find yourself in an unhealthy emotional relationship with another person, what are some of the practical things you can do to set your heart right with God?

- □ *Pray and ask God for forgiveness. Ask him to help you to loosen the unhealthy ties with the person you are emotionally attached to.*
- □ *Be deliberate about finding other people to do things with, and other friendships to cultivate.*
- □ *Break your 'pattern of contact' with this person; make changes.*
- □ *Ask for real-life examples from the group of how someone has overcome an unhealthy emotional attachment to another person.*

Hardening of the Heart

Some people, as a result of past hurts in their lives, have allowed their hearts to turn to stone as a defense mechanism to protect them from further hurt. You can easily tell who they are. This person will

- Almost never smile;
- Have very few friends, if any;
- Have a cold demeanor;
- Appear rude or arrogant; and
- You can hear them say that they don't care what people think about them.

The truth is, they do care what people think about them, but they have been so deeply hurt that they have built up a stone wall around their heart and are hurting so much inside, that they have isolated themselves and put people at a distance to prevent any more pain from coming their way.

The Word of God gives us great hope in knowing that even if we have a stone-cold heart, He can turn your life around and soften your heart once again so that he can pour his pure love into you and revitalize your heart and your spirit. Turn to Ezekiel 36:26.

3. God will take the heart of <u>stone</u> out of your flesh and give you a new heart of <u>flesh</u> (Ezekiel 36:26).

Ezekiel 36:26 - *I will give you a new heart and put a new spirit within you; I will take the heart of stone out of your flesh and give you a heart of flesh.*

<u>Engage the participants in conversation</u>: Ask for volunteers to answer the questions below. If no response is offered, the sub-bullets may provide enough to get the conversation started.

Have you ever personally experienced the heart of stone? Explain.

    □ *If yes, how did you react to other people?*

    □ *What types of things did you repeatedly hear other people say to you or about you?*

    □ *How did you feel inside when others approached you?*

    □ *How was your relationship with God at that time?*

Have you ever known someone else who appeared to have a heart of stone?

Did you try to engage in conversation with that person? Why/why not?

How did they interact with people?

Turn your Bible to Ephesians 3:16-19 and read what Paul is saying to the Ephesian Church and to us.

Ephesians 3:16-19 - *[16]that He would grant you, according to the riches of His glory, to be strengthened with might through His Spirit in the inner man, [17]that Christ may dwell in your hearts through faith; that you, being rooted and grounded in love, [18]may be able to comprehend with all the saints what is the width and length and depth and height ---[19]to know the love of Christ which passes knowledge; that you may be filled with all the fullness of God.*

What does this Scripture say about our hearts?

How can we apply this Scripture to our lives to help us to break unhealthy emotional ties to other man or woman?

Close Out with Prayer

Our Authority in Christ to Rout Demons

LESSON #11

FACILITATOR'S GUIDE

RESOURCES NEEDED FOR THIS CLASS

- Lesson #11 In-Class Discussion Fill in the Blank form (available in Workbook and in the ADDITIONAL CLASSROOM MATERIALS FOR INDIVIDUAL LESSONS Section of this Facilitator Guide)

If you have surrendered your life to Jesus and truly accepted Him as Lord and Savior, you already have the power and authority of Jesus' name to cast out demons and walk in complete victory over the attacks of the enemy.

We read in the Scriptures where Jesus sent His disciples out in pairs and instructed them to heal the sick, cleanse lepers, raise the dead, and cast out demons (Matthew 10:1-4; Mark 6:7; Luke 9:1-3). Jesus taught His disciples saying, "Most assuredly, I say to you, he who believes in Me, the works that I do he will do also; and greater works than these he will do, because I go to My Father. And whatever you ask in My name, that I will do, that the Father may be glorified in the Son. If you ask anything in My name, I will do it." (John 14:12-14). He also teaches us to resist the enemy and draw near to God (James 4:7-8). God is the one who will fight for us.

We are not to fear the enemy. Jesus has already defeated Satan when He was crucified, died, was buried, and rose from the dead, and is now seated at the right hand of the Father in heaven. Jesus will finally cast Satan into the lake of fire for all of eternity at the appointed time (Revelation 20:2-3, 7,10). Furthermore, God's Word assures us that nothing can harm us or separate us from his love.

[35]Who shall separate us from the love of Christ? Shall tribulation, or distress, or persecution, or famine, or nakedness, or peril, or sword? [36]As it is written:

"For Your sake we are killed all day long; We are accounted as sheep for the slaughter."

[37]Yet in all these things we are more than conquerors through Him who loved us. [38]For I am persuaded that neither death nor life, nor angels nor principalities nor powers, nor things present nor things to come, [39]nor height nor depth, nor any other created thing, shall be able to separate us from the love of God which is in Christ Jesus our Lord. (Romans 8:35-39)

This Week's Memory Verse:

James 4:7 (NKJV) *Therefore submit to God. Resist the devil and he will flee from you.*

Break Down the Memory Verse

- What does it mean "Resist the devil"?
- What happens when we resist the devil?

Discussion

Go over the homework assignment and ask participants to share their answers to some of the questions presented.

Fill in the blank Exercise (Located behind this week's homework in the Workbook, and in the appendix to this Facilitator Guide). Or use your imagination as a facilitator to make each lesson interesting and engaging for the participants utilizing some of the ideas presented in the "How to Use This Facilitator Guide" section on page 9.

A couple of weeks ago, we memorized 2 Corinthians 10:3-5. Do you remember that Scripture? Let's read it again and refresh what it says in our memory and in our Spirits.

1. The <u>war</u> we fight and the <u>weapons</u> we use are not of this world, they are <u>spiritual</u> (2 Corinthians 10:3-5).

2. To demolish the <u>strongholds</u> that keep us in bondage to sin, we have to <u>trust</u> God and change our <u>thinking</u> (2 Corinthians 10:3-5).

The Word says we have to take every thought captive to the obedience of Christ. That means any thought that wants to rationalize why it is OK to continue doing what we are doing to satisfy the lusts of the flesh has to be taken into captivity to see if it lines up with the word of God.

2 Corinthians 10:3-5 - *³For though we live in the world, we do not wage war as the world does. ⁴The weapons we fight with are not the weapons of the world. On the contrary, they have divine power to demolish strongholds. ⁵We demolish arguments and every pretension that sets itself up against the knowledge of God, and we take captive every thought to make it obedient to Christ.*

If we are born-again Christians, we are in a spiritual battle whether we like it or not. As soon as we accepted Jesus Christ and turned away from the ways of the world to follow Jesus, a war has been raging inside of us between our spirit and our flesh. The battle has been raging outside of us as well because the devil is mad.

While we fight this battle, we do not do it blindly. We have the enemy's battle plans; in fact, we have been studying them over these past few weeks. We also don't ever have to fight alone! We have Jesus right there beside us fighting this battle if we surrender our lives to Him and allow Him to guide and direct everything we do, holding no parts of our lives back.

Let's look at an example from the Bible where God's children refused to get caught up in the world and what everybody else was doing, but took a stand for God and what He wanted them to do. Turn in the Bible to Daniel Chapter 3. Read Daniel 3:1-30.

What did Shadrach, Meshach, and Abed-Nego refuse to do that got them into trouble with the king?

- *They refused to worship the idol.*

What the Jewish law (the Bible) say about what King Nebuchadnezzar was ordering them to do?

- *The law of Moses prohibits worshipping idols.*

How is this related to ungodly relationships and other areas of bondage that we face today?

- *The world says that all are free to love and enter into intimate and sexual relationships with whomever we choose.*
  - □ *God's word says sexual intimacy outside of marriage between one man and one woman is wrong.*
  - □ *God's word says that sexual conduct is confined to the boundaries of a marriage relationship between one man and one woman.*

What pressures did Shadrach, Meshach, and Abed-Nego face from the world and the enemy?

- *World - they had to go against very strong peer pressure*
- *Enemy - a threat on their lives*

What pressures do you face when you determine to line your life up with the word of God and make changes that isolate you from people you used to be in relationship with?

- *World - very strong peer pressure to conform to the world*
- *Enemy – temptation and lies about the truth*

What did Shadrach, Meshach, and Abed-Nego say to the king in verses 16-18 when he challenged their rebellion towards his decree to worship the idol and when he challenged their God?

- *They said God is able to deliver them from his hand, and even if God chose not to deliver them, they would still serve Him with all of their hearts.*

What would your life look like if you absolutely refused to live your life in bondage to sin? What would have to change?

What happened to Shadrach, Meshach, and Abed-Nego when they trusted God with their whole hearts and refused to compromise their morals?

  - □ *The survived the fiery furnace with absolutely no traces of smoke or fire on them.*
  - □ *They were not alone in the fire – Jesus was right there with them protecting them from harm and delivering them from the hands of the evil king.*

What do you think would happen if you made up in your mind right now that you absolutely will not participate another day in bondage to sin?

Do you think you would have to accomplish this alone? Why/why not?

We know that we are in a spiritual battle. Our resolve to turn away from a life of sin and line our lives up with the word of God makes us a target for the enemy. And we know that the enemy sometimes uses people to try and get us to turn around and satisfy the lusts of the flesh instead of denying those feelings and following God. Turn to 2 Timothy 2:3-4. What does this Scripture say?

3. We are to <u>endure hardship</u> as a good soldier, <u>pleasing</u> to Jesus Christ. (2 Timothy 2:3-4)

    2 Timothy 2:3-4 - ³*You therefore must endure hardship as a good soldier of Jesus Christ. ⁴No one engaged in warfare entangles himself with the affairs of this life, that he may please him who enlisted him as a soldier.*

    What does this Scripture mean practically – as applied to our lives?

    ☐ *It is not easy to deny myself and follow Christ.*
    ☐ *I have to love Jesus more than I love the world.*

    Jesus doesn't leave us by ourselves to fight these battles. What does His word say in 1 John 4:4?

4. I am God's <u>child</u> and have already <u>overcome</u> the enemy because I have God in me and therefore I am <u>stronger</u> than the enemy who is in the world (1 John 4:4).

    1 John 4:4 - *You are of God, little children, and have overcome them, because He who is in you is greater than he who is in the world.*

    Use the remaining time to have the participants share how they are doing in overcoming their bondage to sin by answering the following questions:

    • What changes have you made in your life as a result of these studies that have helped you to break the bondage of sin?
    • What challenges have you faced since you determined to make changes in your life to line it up with the word of God?

Close Out with Prayer

Forgiveness – Part II

FACILITATOR'S GUIDE

RESOURCES NEEDED FOR THIS CLASS

- Lesson #12 In-Class Discussion Fill in the Blank form (available in Workbook and in the ADDITIONAL CLASSROOM MATERIALS FOR INDIVIDUAL LESSONS Section of this Facilitator Guide)

Do you harbor feelings of guilt and self-condemnation for things you have done or failed to do, things that you still struggle with that you know are not pleasing to God, feeling as though your sins are unforgiveable? I have great news for you! Forgiveness is a not a feeling, it is a biblical truth. God's forgiveness is a gift to man as part of our salvation for the blotting out of our transgression's so we can be restored to Him through the shed atoning blood of Jesus Christ. God's forgiveness has erased our sins (past, present, and future) as if they never occurred (Isaiah 43:25-26; Hebrews 10:17; Psalm 103:12, 130:3-4).

This does not mean that after salvation, we will never sin again. God knows our human frailties and therefore He has made provisions for us. When we do mess up and sin, we are to go to God, confess our sins, repent and ask for forgiveness, and He is faithful and just to forgive us and completely cleanse us from all unrighteousness (1 John 1:9). God does not replay the sins that He has forgiven and bring them up against us over and over again. So why are we so hard on ourselves? Why do we feel guilty and condemn ourselves when we sin? Why do we play the movie over and over again in our minds? Maybe it is because it is so hard for us to forgive others and we believe that our imperfect forgiveness of others is equivalent to God's forgiveness of our sins. Or perhaps, it is because we don't fully understand and fully embrace the forgiveness that God has bestowed upon us.

I am not saying that we have to forgive ourselves for our sins. Self-forgiveness is not mentioned in the Bible. Biblical forgiveness is from God to man, and from one man to another. What we need to understand and embrace in order to be free from the guilt and self-condemnation related to our sin is the amazing grace of God. *"Grace perfects forever the saved one in the sight of God because of the saved one's position "in Christ." Grace bestows Christ's merit and Christ's standing forever."* (The *New Unger's Bible Dictionary*, definition of Grace) By grace, we are saved through faith in Jesus Christ (Ephesians 2:8). We can't work for forgiveness or salvation; these are bestowed upon us by the grace of God. We just have to have faith and believe the Word of God, which says that God will forgive our sins when we repent and ask for His forgiveness, and He will blot out the memory of our sin as if it never occurred.

Like I said at the beginning, forgiveness is not a feeling. If you don't 'feel' forgiven for the sins you have committed despite asking God for His forgiveness, you must accept God's forgiveness by faith. Think about the incredibly high price that God paid for the forgiveness of your sins. He sacrificed His one and only son, Jesus Christ, who shed His blood for the remission of your sins (Matthew 26:28; Ephesians 1:7). God will not withhold his forgiveness from you if you truly repent and ask for His forgiveness (1 John 1:9).

This Week's Memory Verse:

Isaiah 43:25-26 (NKJV) *"I, even I, am He who blots out your transgressions for My own sake; And I will not remember your sins. Put Me in remembrance; Let us contend together; State your case, that you may be acquitted."*

Break Down the Memory Verse

- For whose sake does God blot out our transgressions? Why?
- Does it say God forgets your sins? What is the distinction between forgetting and not remembering?
- What does it mean to contend together?
- Acquitted – means cleared from a charge/accusation. Receiving a judgment of "not guilty"

Discussion

Go over the homework assignment and ask participants to share their answers to some of the questions presented.

Fill in the blank Exercise (Located behind this week's homework in the Workbook, and in the appendix to this Facilitator Guide). Or use your imagination as a facilitator to make each lesson interesting and engaging for the participants utilizing some of the ideas presented in the "How to Use This Facilitator Guide" section on page 9.

When God forgives you, you are truly forgiven! How do we know this? Read John 8:36.

1. If Jesus makes you free from your sin, you are free indeed. (John 8:36)

   John 8:36 - *Therefore if the Son makes you free, you shall be free indeed.*

   Jesus paid an incredibly high price to forgive us from our sins and restore our relationship with God. Turn to Ephesians 1:7. What does this passage of Scripture say?

2. We are redeemed by the blood of Jesus and are granted forgiveness of our sins according to the riches of His grace. (Ephesians 1:7)

   Ephesians 1:7 - *In Him we have redemption through His blood, the forgiveness of sins, according to the riches of His grace*

3. While Jesus stands ready to forgive us of our sins, there are some prerequisites to receiving God's forgiveness. What do you suppose they are?

   - Repent – express sincere regret – true change of heart and turning away from sin (Matthew 9:13)
   - Confess – tell God what we are repenting for (1 John 1:9)
   - Ask – we must expressly ask God for forgiveness (1 John 5:14-15, Matthew 21:22)

   Matthew 9:13 - *But go and learn what this means: 'I desire mercy and not sacrifice.' For I did not come to call the righteous, but sinners, to repentance.*

1 John 1:9 - *If we confess our sins, He is faithful and just to forgive us our sins and to cleanse us from all unrighteousness.*

1 John 5:14-15 – *[14]Now this is the confidence that we have in Him, that if we ask anything according to His will, He hears us. [15]And if we know that He hears us, whatever we ask, we know that we have the petitions that we have asked of Him.*

Matthew 21:22 - *And whatever things you ask in prayer, believing, you will receive.*

God's forgiveness is so complete that when we are forgiven, He does something very special for us. Turn to Hebrews 8:12.

4. When Jesus forgives our sins, He chooses <u>not</u> to <u>remember</u> our <u>sin</u>. (Hebrews 8:12)

Hebrews 8:12 - *For I will be merciful to their unrighteousness, and their sins and their lawless deeds I will remember no more.*

This is profoundly demonstrated in the case of King David. Let's turn to 2 Samuel Chapter 11 – read through Chapter 12:15.

David has sinned greatly against God by sleeping with Bathsheba and having Uriah killed. Now, let's move ahead in time to a Scripture where the prophet Ahija is talking to Jeroboam who will become king of the northern kingdom of Israel. He is speaking of Solomon (King David's son) who will retain part of Israel as a result of a promise that God made to David. Pay attention to what the prophet says about King David. Let's turn now to 1 Kings 11:34.

How do you think God can speak through his servant the prophet like this when we all know what David did?

1 Kings 11:34 - *However I will not take the whole kingdom out of his hand, because I have made him ruler all the days of his life for the sake of My servant David, whom I chose because he kept My commandments and My statutes.*

It is important to note that David did not go unpunished for his sin. Let's turn back to 2 Samuel 12:16-23.

There are always consequences for our sin. We can be forgiven, but that does not mean that we are absolved of the effects of our sin.

•   How did David respond to the death of his son?
•   Why do you think David could respond like he did?
•   Do you think your response would have been similar? Why/why not?

5. God stands ready to <u>forgive</u> us, and He is <u>merciful</u> and <u>loving</u> towards us. (Psalm 86:4-5)

Psalm 86:4-5 - *[4]Rejoice the soul of Your servant, For to You, O Lord, I lift up my soul. [5]For You, Lord, are good, and ready to forgive, [5]And abundant in mercy to all those who call upon You.*

But sometimes, we fail to go to God for forgiveness of our sins. As believers, our sin cannot separate us from God, meaning that we cannot lose our salvation, but we will be out of fellowship with God when we have unrepentant sin in our lives.

6. Nothing can <u>separate</u> us from the <u>love</u> of God. (Romans 8:38-39)

Romans 8:38-39 - [38]*For I am persuaded that neither death nor life, nor angels nor principalities nor powers, nor things present nor things to come,* [39]*nor height nor depth, nor any other created thing, shall be able to separate us from the love of God which is in Christ Jesus our Lord.*

Our unrepentant sin results in us being outside the fellowship of God because God is Holy and He cannot remain in the presence of sin. We have the Holy Spirit residing inside us, and therefore, when we deliberately sin and refuse to repent and be forgiven, we will not feel the loving presence of God in our lives in the way we would if our conscience was completely clear.

Engage the participants in discussion:

- Do you now or have you ever had unrepentant sin in your life after salvation?
- What is holding you back from repenting, confessing, and asking God for forgiveness?
- Why do you believe that we are unwilling to go to God for forgiveness?
- Have you added anything this week to your Timeline? If so, what?

Close Out with Prayer

Removing Hindrances to Effective Prayer

FACILITATOR'S GUIDE

RESOURCES NEEDED FOR THIS CLASS

- Small group exercise to identify biblical hindrances to prayer (*Prayer Blockers - Possible Reasons Why Our Prayers are Not Answered by God* Available in Workbook and in the ADDITIONAL CLASSROOM MATERIALS FOR INDIVIDUAL LESSONS Section of this Facilitator Guide)

Prayer is the expression of man's dependence upon God for all things. (The *New Unger's Bible Dictionary*). It is essentially our lifeline to God. It is vitally important then that our prayers are getting through to God, that He hears us and answers our prayers.

The Bible reveals a number of hindrances or barriers to effective prayer, which we will look at this week. If we can identify any of these barriers in our lives, with God's help we can remove them so we can effectively communicate with Him through prayer and receive the blessings and provision that He has for us.

God requires us to be obedient to His Word (1 Samuel 15:22). We can cry out to God day and night in prayer, but if we harbor certain sins in our lives, they will block our communication channel with God, and He will not answer our prayers. Some of the sins that create barriers or hindrances to prayer are: unforgiveness, unbelief, unrepentant sin, asking for things with wrong motives or contrary to the will of God, continued willful sin, pride, hypocrisy, and selfishness.

There are numerous examples where the people of God sinned and as a result, God did not answer their prayers or the prayers of those praying on their behalf. (See Joshua 7:1-12; 2 Samuel 12:13-23; 1 Samuel 14:37; Numbers 20:7-12, 27:14) Elsewhere in the Word of God, we are told explicitly the things that will hinder our prayer life with God.

A healthy vibrant intimate relationship with God requires a clear communication channel between us and God. Let's examine our lives to see where we need to make changes to improve our ability to communicate with and experience intimacy with God, so we can receive the blessings and provision that come to us as a result of prayer.

This Week's Memory Verse:

2 Chronicles 7:14-15 (NKJV) [14]*if My people who are called by My name will humble themselves, and pray and seek My face, and turn from their wicked ways, then I will hear from heaven, and will forgive their sin and heal their land.* [15]*Now My eyes will be open and My ears attentive to prayer made in this place.*

Break Down the Memory Verse

What does God say in our Scripture about the posture we are to take when we come to Him in prayer?

- *Humble self*
- *Seek His face – come to Him with complete honesty*
- *Turn from our wicked ways*

What does He say He will do if we do our part?

- *He will hear us.*
- *He will forgive us.*
- *He will heal us.*
- *His eyes will be open and His ears attentive when we pray to Him 'in this place' – in this posture of humility and honesty.*

Discussion

Go over the homework assignment and ask participants to share their answers to some of the questions presented.

Small Group Exercise (Located behind this week's homework in the Participant Guide, and in the appendix to this Facilitator Guide)

In-Class Small Group Exercise

Small group exercise to identify biblical hindrances to prayer *(Prayer Blockers - Possible Reasons Why Our Prayers are Not Answered by God)*

Have participants work on the exercise together in smaller groups and then report to the class at the end. Answers to the blank right column are provided in this Facilitator Guide below:

Scripture Reference	Hindrance(s) to Effective Prayer
Deuteronomy 1:45 1 Samuel 14:37 1 Samuel 28:6	Disobedience
Proverbs 1:24-28	Indifference
Scripture Reference	Hindrance(s) to Effective Prayer
Proverbs 28:9	Despising the Law, rejection
Isaiah 1:15 Isaiah 59:3	Bloodguiltiness, Blood Shedders

Scripture Reference	Hindrance(s) to Effective Prayer
Isaiah 59:2 Micah 3:4 John 9:31 Psalm 66:18	Iniquity, Living in Sin
Zechariah 7:11-13	Stubbornness
James 1:6,7	Instability, wavering
James 4:3	Self-Indulgence
2 Corinthians 12:8 Exodus 33:20 Ezekiel 20:3	Not in Accordance with God's will
Hosea 5:1-7 Luke 18:11, 12, 14	Arrogant Attitude – self-incriminating and self-destructive; Self-Righteous
Isaiah 1:2-20	Oppressed Others and therefore God would not hear them (read in context 1:2-20)
Proverbs 21:13	Deaf to the Cry of the Poor
Jeremiah 14:10,12	Forsake God
Proverbs 1:24, 25, 28	Reject the Call of God
Jeremiah 11:11-14 Ezekiel 8:15-18	Idolaters
Job 27:8,9	Hypocrites
Job 35:12,13	Pride

Now that we have identified things that hinder our prayers to God, what are the things that enhance our prayers?

Look at the opposite of each thing that hinders prayer to determine what God requires for answered prayer:

- Obedience
- Caring about the things of God
- Love of God's Law

- Honor and protect life
- Despising sin and not practicing it in our lives
- Yielding to the will of God
- Steadfast faith
- Self-control
- Praying in accordance with God's will
- Meekness
- Being gracious towards others
- Helping the poor
- Holding fast to God
- Heeding the call of God and immediately obeying Him
- No other 'gods' in our lives. Complete devotion to the one and only God
- Integrity
- Humility

Let's look at a notable prayer in the Bible and see how many of the positive attributes can we find in this prayer and if this man that made his prayer acceptable to God.

Let's turn to Nehemiah chapter 1. Read the whole chapter.

What do you see about Nehemiah and his prayer to God that reflects what we have learned about prayer that God will answer?

- ☐ *Caring about the things of God (v.3) - Nehemiah had God's heart towards the people and the city of God (Jerusalem)*
- ☐ *Love of God's Law (v.7)*
- ☐ *Honor and protect life (v.3)*
- ☐ *Despising sin and not practicing it in our lives (v. 6-7)*
- ☐ *Yielding to the will of God (v.4-5)*
- ☐ *Steadfast faith (v.5)*
- ☐ *Self-control (v.4)*
- ☐ *Praying in accordance with God's will*
- ☐ *Meekness (v.7)*
- ☐ *Being gracious towards others*
- ☐ *Helping the poor*
- ☐ *Holding fast to God*
- ☐ *Heeding the call of God and immediately obeying Him*
- ☐ *No other 'gods' in our lives. Complete devotion to the one and only God*
- ☐ *Integrity*
- ☐ *Humility*

Engage the participants in discussion:

Do you recognize any of the prayer blockers in your life?

If so, what will you do to remove them from your life so God will answer your prayers?

Have you added anything this week to your Timeline? If so, what?

Close Out with Prayer

Holy Spirit's Power for Inner Healing and Sanctification

LESSON #14

FACILITATOR'S GUIDE

RESOURCES NEEDED FOR THIS CLASS

- Completed Homework
- Ministry Evaluation Forms for completion during break next week (located in FORMS section of Facilitator Guide)

Who or what is the Holy Spirit? I believe that this member of the Godhead is the least known and understood. We seem to have a much better understanding about God the Father and God the Son (Jesus) than we do about God the Holy Spirit. Let's learn about this powerful helper/counselor that has been freely given to every believer who has accepted Jesus Christ as Lord and Savior to guide our daily lives and transform us from the inside out.

There are several instances in the Bible when all three persons of the Trinity are mentioned together (Matthew 3:16-17; Matthew 28:19; 2 Corinthians 13:14; Titus 3:4-6). The most notable instance is when Jesus was baptized in the Jordan River by John the Baptist *"When He had been baptized, Jesus* [God the Son] *came up immediately from the water; and behold, the heavens were opened to Him, and He saw the Spirit of God* [God the Holy Spirit] *descending like a dove and alighting upon Him. And suddenly a voice came from heaven* [God the Father], *saying, "This is My beloved Son, in whom J am well pleased."* (Matthew 3:16-17)

The Holy Spirit (or Holy Ghost) is a person, not an amorphous 'it'. He is God. In Acts 5:3-4 Peter said *"Ananias, why has Satan filled your heart to lie to the Holy Spirit ... you have not lied to men but to God."*

The Holy Spirit has a very critical role to play in drawing unsaved people towards God for salvation. First, He protects us from being destroyed by Satan until we make a decision to accept Jesus Christ (Isaiah 59:19). Secondly, He convicts us by exposing our sin to us, so we know that we need a Savior (John 16:7-8). Finally, He regenerates us by bringing our spirit to life and giving us a new nature the moment we accept Jesus Christ as Lord and Savior (John 3:3-7, 2 Corinthians 5:17).

After we are saved, and the Holy Spirit resides in us, He begins the lifelong work of helping us to live the way God wants us to live. Our bodies become the temple of the Holy Spirit (1 Corinthians 6:19) and He strengthens us for Christian living (Ephesians 3:16). He fills us with His presence if we allow Him the freedom to fill us (Ephesians 5:18). He teaches believers all about spiritual things as we inquire of Him for assistance in understanding God's Word and His ways (John 14:26; 1 John 2:24-27). He gives spiritual gifts to God's children to be used to serve the body of Christ (1 Corinthians 12:1-11; Ephesians 4:12). He also produces fruit in us that demonstrates our love of God and our transformation from carnal to spiritual (Galatians 5:22-23).

In addition to all of the things listed above, the Holy Spirit also performs a life-long process of sanctification where we are healed and changed from the inside out (Romans 15:16; 2 Thessalonians 2:13). Sanctification requires a separation from the secular and sinful and setting apart for a sacred purpose (The *New Unger's Bible Dictionary*).

One important thing to know is that the Holy Spirit is a gentleman. He will not force change on you. But if you yield your will to Him and ask Him to help you, the Holy Spirit will expose areas of sin in your life so you can take those to God and seek His forgiveness, and turn away from that sin and begin living in accordance with God's will for your life. The Holy Spirit lives inside you as a born-again believer, and He has a direct connection to God the Father and God the Son. Isn't that an awesome thought? The Word of God says that He intercedes for us. He is your ultimate prayer partner! (Romans 8:26-27)

The Holy Spirit will also reveal areas of deep-rooted pain in your life, which is a result of injuries that you have buried deep within your soul. In order for you to heal from these things, you have to allow Him to show you the root of problem – where it originated. Once the Spirit of God reveals this to you, take that painful incident to Jesus for healing. You may need to forgive someone for hurting you, or take other actions that the Holy Spirit will reveal to you. Sometimes, we bury things so deeply that we don't even recall being hurt because we have blocked it out of our memory. If you want to be healthy physically and spiritually, you can't hold onto the pain you have buried in your soul. It has to be exposed to the light of the truth of God and released to Him for you to obtain complete healing and deliverance.

The Holy Spirit is a powerful advocate and counselor who is standing by to work mightily in your life if you will allow Him to do what He excels at. And that is to - help you to turn away from sin in your life, and to heal from past sin and pain that you are holding on to so you can fully manifest the fruit of the Spirit in your life.

This Week's Memory Verse:

Romans 8:26-27 (NKJV) [26]*Likewise the Spirit also helps in our weaknesses. For we do not know what we should pray for as we ought, but the Spirit Himself makes intercession for us with groanings which cannot be uttered.* [27]*Now He who searches the hearts knows what the mind of the Spirit is, because He makes intercession for the saints according to the will of God.*

Break Down the Memory Verse

How does the Spirit help us in our weakness?

Have you ever experienced the Holy Spirit praying for you through groanings?

What does it mean to allow the Holy Spirit to search our hearts?

Why is it helpful to allow the Holy Spirit to search our hearts?

Discussion

Go over the homework assignment and ask participants to share their answers to some of the questions presented.

- Facilitate sharing.

□ *Note this class we will delve deeply into the homework assignment and the experience of the participants in completing the assignment*

Engage the participants in discussion

- Ask the participants to review their timelines (Lesson #6) that they have been working on for several weeks now.
- Share what they are discovering about the root causes of their life controlling sinful behaviors.
- Share what the Holy Spirit is revealing about what needs to happen for them to heal from the results of sinful choices in their lives.

Close Out with Prayer

Listening and Inner Healing Prayer

FACILITATOR'S GUIDE

RESOURCES NEEDED FOR THIS CLASS

- Completed homework
- For the facilitator it is helpful to have read *Listening and Inner-Healing Prayer: Meeting God in the Broken Places* by Rusty Rustenbach (NavPress, 2011)

Prayer is how we communicate with God and one of the most powerful ways that He communicates with us. One form of prayer that has the ability to completely transform your life and deepen your intimacy with the Lord is Listening and Inner Healing Prayer. This week we will learn the principles of this type of prayer and put into practice what we learn through guided inner healing prayer sessions.

Jesus came into the world to set us free from sin and the effects of sin in our lives. We read in Luke 4:16-21 that Jesus went into the synagogue in Nazareth and read from the scroll of Isaiah chapter 61 verse 1 (our memory scripture for this week), and when He had finished reading the passage, He said, "The Scripture you've just heard has been fulfilled this very day." (Luke 4:21). What Jesus was saying, is that God sent Him to heal our broken hearts, to give liberty to those captive and in bondage to sin, and to open the prisons in our minds that are constructed by Satan to keep us in bondage.

God wants an intimate relationship with you and He wants to heal all areas of brokenness in your life. He wants you to learn to trust Him and to bring all of your cares and concerns to Him in prayer. In previous lessons, we learned about communicating with God in prayer, and we learned some of the things that hinder our ability to communicate with God. This week we will learn how to sit quietly before God and allow Him to speak to us. There is nothing more important for our spiritual growth than being able to discern the voice of God and to allow Him to speak into our lives.

Each day this week we will be practicing principles of Listening and Inner Healing Prayer. You should plan to set aside at least 30 minutes each day where you can get away from all distractions and be ready to write down what God says to you. I pray that God will speak healing words to you that will transform your life and ignite a passion in your soul to continue to make Listening prayer a regular practice in your life as you continue to grow spiritually in your relationship with Jesus

This Week's Memory Verse

Isaiah 61:1 (NKJV) *The Spirit of the Lord God is upon Me, Because the Lord has anointed Me To preach good tidings to the poor; He has sent Me to heal the brokenhearted, To proclaim liberty to the captives, And the opening of the prison to those who are bound;*

Break Down the Memory Verse

What does it mean to proclaim liberty to the captives?

How can we be imprisoned and in bondage by the enemy?

Note to the Facilitator

Portions of a book titled *Listening and Inner-Healing Prayer: Meeting God in the Broken Places* by Rusty Rustenbach, (NavPress, 2011) was used in the development of this lesson. This book walks you through the process of learning to listen to God for healing in prayer. The second half of the book can be used by a facilitator to guide others through Listening and Inner Healing Prayer. A link to purchase this book and other resources to help facilitate Listening prayer can be found on Debora's website at http://www.DBarrMinistries.org

In-Class Discussion

Go over the week's assignment and engage the participants in discussion about what God is revealing to each of them.

Ask each person to share about their experiences with Listening prayer this week guided by the questions below

- Where did you go to sit quietly before the Lord?
- How did you quiet your mind? Was this difficult for you?
- What frustrations did you experience this week in attempting Listening prayer?
- In what ways did God speak to you?
- How do you know that God was speaking to you?
- Does what you believe you heard align with God's character as revealed in Scripture?
- Will you please share something with the group that God spoke to you?

If there is time at the end of class discussions, you may want to lead the group in a guided session of listening prayer following the guidelines below

- Play quiet instrumental music to set the atmosphere for listening
- Ask each participant to have pen and paper ready to write down anything that God might say to them
- Remind them to be open to any way in which God may wish to communicate with them, surrendering all expectations about what it might be like
- Pray for the group – asking Jesus to speak to each one individually in this time of Listening prayer
- After the allotted time, begin a final prayer thanking God for what He communicated to each person
- If there is time at the end, ask participants to share anything that they wish to share about this Listening prayer session.

The Power of Sharing Your Testimony

LESSON #16

FACILITATOR'S GUIDE

RESOURCES NEEDED FOR THIS CLASS

- Sample Video Testimonies (search the Internet for Testimonies of life transformation as a result of surrendering to the Lordship of Jesus Christ).

There is great power in the telling and hearing of a personal testimony regarding what God is doing and has done in a person's life. Testimony is defined as a declaration by a witness under oath, as that given before a court or deliberative body; evidence in support of a fact or an assertion; or a public declaration regarding a religious experience *(The American Heritage Dictionary of the English Language)*. The Bible is full of stories about what God did in the lives of His people thousands of years ago, but don't you agree that it is a bit hard to relate to some of these stories of people who lived in a far different time, place, and culture than our own?

What if you heard from someone today, who you know and who lives right where you live, about something incredible that God did in his or her life? What if someone you know was healed of an "incurable" disease? Wouldn't that have a stronger impact on you than reading about King Hezekiah being healed from the disease that was supposed to kill him around 700 years before Jesus was born? (Isaiah Chapter 38) What about the testimony of a woman in your town who was barren for years, prayed fervently and then was able to conceive and have a child? Wouldn't her story have a much more powerful impact on you than reading about Hannah in the Bible who lived approximately 1,000 years before Christ? (1 Samuel Chapter 1) What about hearing the personal testimony of a man or woman who lived for years as a gay man or lesbian, and who, through the power of God working in and through their lives, has walked away from that lifestyle, and is now living free from that bondage?

Sharing a personal testimony brings healing and encouragement not only to the person hearing the testimony, but also the person sharing it. For the person sharing, it "seals it" and makes it more real even to them. Sometimes, we can go through something incredible in an almost 'out of body' experience where it doesn't become real and tangible to us until we hear ourselves telling the story, or see a video, or hear someone else tell it. Sharing a testimony also reminds the teller of what God did in his/her life, when in the future, they may be discouraged about something. Just remembering what God has already done in your life can encourage you to hold on when the going gets rough. If He did it before, He can do it again!

Personal testimonies can reach some people for God like nothing else can. To see living tangible proof of the power of God working in a person's life today might just be the thing that leads someone to Christ. And, by the way... Satan hates it!

This Week's Memory Verse:

Revelation 12:11 (NKJV) *And they <u>overcame him</u> by the blood of the Lamb and by the word of their testimony, and they did not love their lives to the death.*

NOTE TO FACILITATOR: Plan to provide samples of video testimony in class this week. You can find such videos on the Internet by searching for life transforming Christian testimonies.

It is important to acknowledge that different participants in the ministry are in different stages of their healing journey. You can encourage each person to think about where they were when they first joined the ministry and how far they have changed or grown since they began their participation. Encourage them to avoid comparing themselves with any other participant in the group.

Break Down the Memory Verse

Who did they '<u>overcome</u>' by the blood of the Lamb and by the word of their testimony?

- □ *Satan*

What do you think the Scripture is referring to when it says "<u>and they did not love their lives to the death</u>"?

- □ They died to self, not denying Jesus even when it cost them their lives instead of living their lives apart from God.
- □ Today, we are to 'die to self' daily (Matthew 16:24, Luke 9:23.)

Discussion

Take some time going over the homework assignment and ask participants to share their answers to the questions presented. Facilitate sharing.

- *Make sure that each person gets an opportunity to share their "Salvation Testimony" (Day 2 Question #5)*
- *Be sure to discuss the question below: (Day 3 Question #4)*

Names in the Bible have great significance. In Joshua 24:11, we see a list of names of the 'peoples' that came against the Israelites. The names of the seven 'peoples' that were conquered by the Israelites, are seven 'spirits' that had to be conquered by the Israelites so they could acquire what God promised them. What deeper meaning is revealed in this passage about what the Israelites faced when they crossed into the Promised Land?

NAME	MEANING	ATTRIBUTES
Amorites	Mountain People	Obsession with earthly fame/glory
Perizzites	Belonging to a Village	Limited vision, laziness, low self-esteem
Canaanites	Lowlands People	Addictions, perversions, people pleasing
Hittites	Sons of Terror/Break Down	Phobias, terror, depression, deceit
Girgashites	Clay dwellers	Focus on earthliness and unbelief

Hivites	Villagers	Vision limited to earthly inheritance
Jebusites	Threshers/Humiliate	Legalism, suppression of spiritual authority

Taken from http://shamah-elim.info (Shamah-Elim Bible Studies)

Show Video Testimonies and engage the participants in discussion following each example

- What stood out to you about this testimony?
- What made it effective/ineffective?
- Did you see/hear something that you would incorporate into your testimony when sharing with others?

Power of Sharing Your Testimony Publicly

- Makes it real for you
- Increases accountability
- Helps you to heal – purging the poison out of your system
- Helps others (encouragement – that they are not alone in their pain)

Close Out with Prayer

Exposing the Pain and Glorifying God

LESSON #17

FACILITATOR'S GUIDE

RESOURCES NEEDED FOR THIS CLASS

- None

Part of our healing comes from exposing our hurts, pains, and embarrassments instead of burying them. Just like a wound that needs to be opened up and flushed out to purge an infection, wounds that we have experienced in our lives due to things we have done or things that have happened to us need to be opened up and dealt with for complete healing. If we keep these hurts and pains buried, they are buried alive and continue to affect us both physically and spiritually. An important part of our healing process is being able to talk about what we have experienced and how we have been affected by it.

The most effective way to begin healing from your wounds is to spend time in prayer with God, talking to Him about what happened. Like we experienced in our times of listening and healing prayer, God will help you to understand how much He loves you, that He was there when you were hurt, and He will help you to heal if you are willing to expose your pains to Him. Just like a child who falls and skins his knee, run to Abba Father and show Him your pain so He can comfort you and heal your wounds.

Another important way that we find healing from the things we have experienced in our lives is to share those experiences and their effect on us with other believers. Spiritual growth is accelerated by our relationships with other Christians. How many times have you been encouraged in your own walk with God when another believer shared with you something that they went through, and how God helped them through it? We learn about faith and experience spiritual growth by interacting with other believers.

There are many instances in the Bible where we see God enabling believers to encourage one another and be transparent with one another about their real struggles. A few of these passages follow: Hebrews 10:24-25; Matthew 18:20; Romans 7:15-25; and James 5:16. If you hold on to your hurts and are not transparent about your experiences and pains, you are masking the truth and may hinder another person's spiritual growth, in addition to delaying your own healing. It is easy for a person who has buried their own pain to believe that they are the only one who has faced what they have experienced. If nobody else is talking about what they have experienced, they may feel all alone in their pain. Once it is exposed to the light, healing begins.

Won't you commit this week to experience healing in some area of your life by exposing an unhealed pain, talking to God about it, and being transparent with another Christian believer about what you have gone through?

This Week's Memory Verse:

James 5:16 (NKJV) *Confess your trespasses to one another, and pray for one another, that you may be healed. The effective, fervent prayer of a righteous man avails much.*

Break Down the Memory Verse

What does it mean to confess?

- [ ] *Acknowledge openly*

What are trespasses?

- [ ] *Lapse or deviation from truth and uprightness*
- [ ] *Sin*
- [ ] *Misdeed*

What does it mean to be healed?

- [ ] *Cure*
- [ ] *Make whole*

Why do you think that confessing our trespasses/pains/failings to one another helps to bring healing?

- [ ] *Exposes pain to the light*
- [ ] *It brings it up out of the recesses of our hearts*
- [ ] *Buried pain is buried alive and can't be healed until exposed*

Discussion

Ask each participant if they took the challenge to experience healing in some are of their life and ask them to share what happened.

- What did God reveal to you during your time of prayer?
- Did opportunities open up for you to share your testimony with someone else, and did you share?
- If yes, what did you share?
- What was the effect on you and on the other person?
- If you didn't share, why didn't you share?

Go over the homework assignment in detail asking participants to share their answers to the questions presented. Facilitate sharing.

In-Class Exercise (if have at least 30 minutes remaining)

- Take 3-5 minutes and think about the first time you experienced a life-controlling sinful behavior.
- Write down what triggered it, what someone else did, what you did, how it made you feel, and what you now know about the root cause(s) of these feelings.

- After knowing all you know now about what that experience opened up in your life, how would you warn a friend who reveals to you that he/she is experiencing a similar situation?
- Pair up with a partner and share your testimony (5 minutes for each person to share).

After sharing in pairs (or if the class is very small, each person can share with the group)

- Is this the first time you have ever shared that story with anyone?
- How did it feel to organize your thoughts about what happened and share it publicly?
- Do you think it will be easier to share your story again with someone if the opportunity comes up in the future?

Close Out with Prayer

Tailoring Your Message for the Listener

LESSON #18

FACILITATOR'S GUIDE

RESOURCES NEEDED FOR THIS CLASS

- Lesson #18 In-Class Exercise (available in Workbook and in the ADDITIONAL CLASSROOM MATERIALS FOR INDIVIDUAL LESSONS Section of this Facilitator Guide)

God uses people and their stories to draw others to Himself. Think about it: has anyone in your life ever shared his or her faith with you? If you are like most people, you heard the Gospel message more than once from several different people before you responded and accepted Jesus Christ for yourself.

In addition to drawing people to the saving knowledge of Jesus Christ through the sharing of the Gospel, God uses the stories of His impact on ordinary everyday people to give others hope, to increase their faith, and to bring them comfort. When we hear about what God miraculously did for someone else when we are in the midst of a struggle, or in the midst of pain and suffering, it may be just what we need to hold on a little longer and to actually believe it could happen for us, too!

God is working in the lives of his children – all of them – including you. He does not want you to keep to yourself what He has done in your life. He wants you to share it with others. He loves to hear His children talking about what an incredible God He is and what He has done for them. Think about how good it feels to hear someone talking to someone else about what a good friend you are, what a good parent you are, and what great things you have done for them.

When we share what God has done in our lives, we need to tailor the message to the listener. What I mean is the story of what God did for you doesn't change, but in order to communicate that well, you need to modify the story a bit to get the message across in the most powerful and effective way to various audiences.

Here is an example. When sharing your salvation testimony with someone who has never been in a church before, it would be ineffective to use "church" words like salvation, saved, blood of the Lamb, etc. because they won't know what you are talking about and may think you are a little crazy. It is much more effective to just tell the story using everyday words that they can understand, like "I used to live a self-centered life. I was never satisfied and always wondered why I was even here. I discovered that I was a sinner and that my sins were separating me from God. That is when I met Jesus. He died to take away my sins and to restore my relationship with God. I asked Jesus for forgiveness and He restored me to God and my whole life has changed! I now have a peace that I never knew before..." You get the idea?

We also need to be careful to tailor our testimony to listeners based on their age, their maturity level, etc. This is especially important when sharing your deliverance testimony. Only include the details that are appropriate for the listener. This week, we will study various instances where Paul shared his testimony to get some insight on how to do this.

This Week's Memory Verse:

1 Corinthians 9:22 (NKJV) *to the weak I became as weak, that I might win the weak. I have become all things to all men, that I might by all means save some.*

Break Down the Memory Verse

What is Paul communicating to us in this passage about how he tailored his message?

☐ *He "spoke the language" of the people he was trying to reach*

What was Paul's purpose in becoming like those he was witnessing to?

☐ *He was trying to save them*

How does this passage relate to what we studied this week?

☐ *We need to tailor our message to our listeners to have the greatest impact*

Discussion

Go over the homework assignment in detail and ask participants to share their answers to some of the questions presented. Facilitate sharing.

In-Class Exercise (if have at least 30-45 minutes remaining) **(Located behind this week's homework in the Participant Workbook, and in the appendix to this Facilitator Guide)**

- Ask each participant to mentally identify one family member or friend who they know is not saved.
- Now, suppose that person walks up and asks him/her why he/she believes in Jesus, what difference has it made in his/her life?
- Have them take a few minutes and think about what they would say to that person. Jot down a few notes, if needed.

Give each participant an opportunity to practice what he/she would say to his/her family member or friend by saying it to a partner (or if the class is small – to the whole group).

- Set up chairs facing each other. Let the "friend/family member" surrogate sit in one chair and the participant who will share his/her testimony in the other chair.
- The surrogate should ask questions.

After each participant shares his/her testimony and answers the questions asked by the surrogate:

- How did it feel to share your testimony in this way?
- Do you feel you could do this if that person came up to you and asked you the question tomorrow?
- What can you do to strengthen your testimony?

Close Out with Prayer

Spiritual Gifts and Calling

LESSON #19

FACILITATOR'S GUIDE

RESOURCES NEEDED FOR THIS CLASS

- Spiritual Gifts Inventory. Search the Internet for "Spiritual Gifts Inventory" or "Spiritual Gifts Assessment", or you can find different assessment tools at Christian bookstores.

There are a variety of Spiritual Gifts listed in the Bible. Some are considered supernatural manifestations of the Holy Spirits' work through a believer; others are motivational gifts; and still others are considered ministry gifts. Regardless of what you call them or how they are displayed in a believer's life, they are all given to us by God and are to be used in service to other people and to bring glory and honor to the One who gave them to us.

The church is sometimes described in terms of the people who make up the various parts of the body. (See 1 Corinthians Chapter 12.) Each person in the body of Christ has a role to play using the gifts that God has equipped him or her with. No gift is more important than any other. Just as every part of the physical body is important, and the body doesn't function well when a part is missing or is not operating to its full potential, the Body of Christ needs each and every member operating in the gift that has been given by God to be healthy and whole.

This week, you will take a Spiritual Gifts Survey to determine what gifts you have been equipped with so you can begin to learn about your gifts and how you can use them to serve others. You can find Spiritual Gifts Surveys on the Internet or in Christian Bookstores. If you are not already using your Spiritual Gifts in service to the Body of Christ, make a commitment this week to learn more about your gifts and to use them as God intended. You will be blessed when you are operating in the center of God's will – and that includes operating and functioning in the unique gifting that has been given to you in service to others.

This Week's Memory Verse:

1 Peter 4:10 (NKJV) *As each one has received a gift, <u>minister it to one another, as good stewards of the manifold grace of God</u>.*

NOTE TO FACILITATOR: In this lesson, the participants need to complete a Spiritual Gifts Inventory as part of their homework assignment. Search the Internet for "Spiritual Gifts Inventory" or "Spiritual Gifts Assessment" or you can find different assessment tools at Christian bookstores. Regardless of the source of the assessment tool, you will be able to facilitate the in-class portion of this exercise following the outline below.

Break Down the Memory Verse

What does Paul mean when he says "minister it to one another"?

      ☐ *Serve others using your gift*

What does it mean to be "a good steward of the manifold grace of God"?

      ☐ *To be a good manager/superintendent (Steward)*

      ☐ *Various sorts (manifold)*

      ☐ *Good will; loving kindness; merciful kindness (grace)*

Discussion

Go over the homework assignment in detail and ask participants to share their answers to the questions presented. Facilitate sharing.

Day 1 Homework

- Ask participants to share the results of their Spiritual Gifts Survey
  - ☐ Were you surprised at the results?

Day 2 Homework

Manifestation Gifts (1 Corinthians 12:1-11)
Discover Your God-Given Gifts by Don & Katie Fortune (Chosen Books 2009), p. 16.

- **The Word of Wisdom** – a revelation of wisdom beyond natural human wisdom that enables a person to know what to do or say
- **The Word of Knowledge** – a revelation of information for a person, group or situation that could not have been known by any natural means
- **Faith** – the kind of wonder-working faith that moves mountains and waits expectantly for results
- **Gifts of Healing** – the many different ways and varieties of degrees in which God manifests healing
- **Working of Miracles** – the demonstration of the power and action of God that goes beyond natural laws
- **Prophecy** – an anointed proclamation of God through an individual to encourage, exhort or comfort
- **Discerning of Spirits** – a person's ability to perceive what type of spirit is in operation in a given situation
- **Various kinds of Tongues** – the languages directed to God, given to the believer by the Holy Spirit but not learned or understood by the speaker
- **Interpretation of Tongues** – the supernatural ability to express the content of what has been spoken in tongues

The PURPOSE of these gifts is to profit the body of believers (not the individual exhibiting the gift).

The SOURCE of these gifts is the Holy Spirit (verses 4, 5, and 11), and there is nothing a believer can do to "get" these gifts – they are feely distributed by the Holy Spirit (v.11).

Day 3 Homework

Motivational Gifts (Romans 12:3-8)

Discover Your God-Given Gifts by Don & Katie Fortune (Chosen Books 2009), p. 18-19.

- **Perceiver** – one who clearly perceives the will for God
- **Server** – one who loves to serve others, a 'doer'
- **Teacher** – one who loves to research and communicate truth
- **Exhorter** – one who loves to encourage others to live a victorious life, encourager
- **Giver** – one who loves to give time, talent, energy and means to benefit others to advance the Gospel, contributor
- **Administrator** – one who loves to organize, lead, or direct, facilitator, leader
- **Compassion Person** – one who shows compassion, love and care to those in need

Discuss how these gifts are ever present in each person's life. They may use them in their profession, and personal life in addition to ministry.

Day 4 Homework

Ministry Gifts (Ephesians 4:7-16)
Discover Your God-Given Gifts by Don & Katie Fortune (Chosen Books 2009), p. 17.

- **Apostle** – one who establishes and strengthens churches
- **Prophet** – one who speaks forth the message of God
- **Evangelist** – one who is called to preach the Gospel
- **Pastor** – one who feeds and shepherds the believers
- **Teacher** – one who instructs believers in the Word of God

These ministry gifts are given by Jesus for the equipping of the saints and for the work of ministry – to edify the body of Christ (verses 11-12).

Day 5 Homework

Various Gifts (1 Corinthians 12:28-30)
Discover Your God-Given Gifts by Don & Katie Fortune (Chosen Books 2009), p. 21.

Motivational Gifts	Ministry Gifts	Manifestation Gifts
Helps (serving)	Apostles	Miracles
Administration	Prophets	Healings
	Teachers	Tongues
		Interpretation

Ask the participants to share their combinations of gifts and how they know they possess these gifts.

- Have the participants discuss various ways in which they can use their gifts to serve in ministry.
- Help each person make a commitment to get connected in such a way that they can begin to exercise their spiritual gifts.

Close Out with Prayer

Witnessing – The Great Commission

FACILITATOR'S GUIDE

RESOURCES NEEDED FOR THIS CLASS

- Bema Judgment Seat of Christ Drama – This drama is available on YouTube via a link from http://www.dbarrministries.org on the Ministry Resources page

After Jesus was raised from the dead and appeared to his disciples, He commissioned them to make disciples of all the nations. He told them to baptize believers in the name of the Father and of the Son and of the Holy Spirit, teaching believers to observe all of the things He had commanded them.

Jesus also calls us to make disciples by sharing the great news of the Gospel with unbelievers. Every believer is commanded by Jesus to share the Gospel with unbelievers (Matthew 28:19; Mark 16:15; Luke 24:47; and John 20:21). This is not just a job for Pastors and Ministers. You and I are to share the Gospel as well, and the Holy Spirit will enable you to share it with His power (Acts 1:8).

Do you remember who led you to Christ? Perhaps you heard a sermon or read a book that pricked your heart, or maybe someone shared the good news with you one-on-one. One way to lead a person to Christ is to follow a series of Scriptures known as the "Romans Road." The book of Romans lays out the Gospel message in an easy to understand story.

The Romans Road story begins by revealing the current state of the unsaved. We are all born into sin as a result of the sin of Adam and Eve in the Garden of Eden. The story goes on to reveal the demonstration of the amazing love of Jesus Christ for all men, that while we were still living in sin, Jesus Christ died on the cross to take away the sins of the world. The only requirement for a man to be saved is to accept the free gift of salvation offered by God. There is absolutely nothing man can do to earn a right to be called a child of God and to earn salvation and eternal life. This is a free gift offered by God to any person who recognizes the sacrificial death of Jesus, and who believes by faith alone that Jesus died for them. When that person calls on the name of the Lord Jesus Christ, he/she WILL be saved.

This is the great news of the Gospel. Every child of God is commanded to share this Good News with others. This week, we will study the Scriptures associated with the Romans Road and learn to share the Gospel as God commands us.

This Week's Memory Verse:

Matthew 28:19-20 (NKJV) [19]*Go therefore and make disciples of all the nations, baptizing them in the name of the Father and of the Son and of the Holy Spirit,* [20]*teaching them to observe all things that I have commanded you; and lo, I am with you always, even to the end of the age.*" Amen.

Break Down the Memory Verse

What are the three steps Jesus identified for us to follow to make disciples?

- ☐ *Go – requires action on behalf of believers*
- ☐ *Baptize – lead them to Christ, demonstrated by physical baptism*
- ☐ *Teach – teach them the ways and commands of God*

What is Jesus' promise to us when we obey the Great Commission?

- ☐ *He will be with us always – we are not doing this in our own power!*

Discussion

Due to time constraints if using the BEMA Judgment Seat of Christ Drama in class, briefly ask each participant to share their experiences in practicing the Romans Road method of sharing the Gospel – asking for any testimonies where they actually used this method to lead someone to Christ.

BEMA Judgment Seat of Christ Drama by Pete Briscoe

A powerful story that will demonstrate the practical application and eternal results of the lesson that was taught this week, is a drama by Pastor Pete Briscoe (Bent Tree Bible Church in Texas) where he walks us through a presentation of what worship at the BEMA judgment seat will be like when we see Christ face to face.

Bema Judgment Seat of Christ Drama – This drama is available on YouTube via a link from http://www.dbarrministries.org on the Ministry Resources page

The presentation lasts 1 hour and 10 minutes.

Some reference Scriptures related to the Bema Judgment Seat of Christ Drama:

Resurrection Bodies – 1 Cor 15:35 - 58; 1 Cor 15:49 ; Rom 8:23, 1 Cor 15:25 - 28, 1 John 3:2

Works judged – 1 Cor 3:12 - 15

Christians will also be judged – 1 Cor. 4:5; 2 Cor 5:1 - 10; Phil 3:21; Rev 21:4; Matt 16:27; Rom 14:10 - 12

Glorification – 1 John 3:2; Rom 8:18 - 19,30

Close Out with Prayer

Your Life's Purpose

FACILITATOR'S GUIDE

RESOURCES NEEDED FOR THIS CLASS

- Sample Mission/Vision Statement for Facilitator

God has a plan and a purpose for your life. In addition to your personal deliverance and healing from the wounds associated with your bondage to sin, God wants to use you and your testimony to bring other people to the saving knowledge of Him. He created you, loves you, and has been preparing you for your Mission your whole life (Ephesians 2:10).

Just like Paul and many others in the Bible, God will use the story of your life to bring glory and honor to Him as you are obedient to do what He reveals to you. When we look outside our own lives and see our circumstances from God's eye view, we can see that He has been preparing us all of our lives to come to know and serve Him. Isaiah 55:8-9 says, *"For My thoughts are not your thoughts, nor are your ways My ways, says the Lord. For as the heavens are higher than the earth, so are My ways higher than your ways, and My thoughts than your thoughts."* God sees the big picture and knows exactly how He wants you to serve Him.

This week, you will write your personal Mission and Vision Statements. You will also revisit your personal timeline (Lesson #6), and instead of focusing on the past, you will project your timeline into the future to show the steps necessary to achieve the Vision God will reveal to you. There is power in writing down what God reveals to you. Just like the power of the written Word in the Bible, writing down the truth that God reveals to you as you pray and ask Him to show you how He wants to use your life, is the first step to seeing those plans displayed in your life.

Writing and continuously reviewing your personal Mission and Vision statements also helps you to stay focused on the things that God has uniquely gifted and equipped you to contribute as part of the Body of Christ. There are numerous 'good things' that you can be doing, but if they distract from the Mission and Vision that God has revealed to you, you will be less effective, and may get burned out. After you have your clear Mission and Vision from God, evaluate every opportunity that comes your way and see if it will advance or detract from what He has assigned you to do. Only participate in activities that move you closer to your Mission and Vision.

Please know that we are not saved by the works that we do for God. "For by grace you have been saved through faith, and that not of yourselves; *it is* the gift of God, not of works, lest anyone should boast." (Ephesians 2:8-9) Our salvation comes from the finished work of Jesus Christ and our faith in Him alone. The works that we do are a natural response to the amazing gift of salvation given to us by Jesus Christ, and the Word tells us that our faith without works is dead (James 2:14-26).

It is important that you don't miss a single day of the homework this week. You will be producing a personal Mission and Vision statement that you will bring to class to share with the others at the conclusion of this lesson, along with the new things God has revealed for you to add to your timeline (Lesson #6).

This Week's Memory Verse:

Ephesians 2:10 (NKJV) *For we are His <u>workmanship</u>, created in Christ Jesus for <u>good works</u>, which God prepared beforehand that we should walk in them.*

Break Down the Memory Verse

Workmanship

- ☐ *That which God created, that which God has made*

Good works

- ☐ *God gifts us for service to Him – these gifts are not of ourselves, but by the grace of God are given to us to serve the Body of Christ*

Discussion

Go over the homework assignment in detail and ask participants to share their answers to the questions presented. Facilitate sharing.

Mission and Vision Statements

Ask each participant to share his/her Mission and Vision Statement that they developed this week along with the scriptural references associated. Have him/her present it to the class in whatever format he/she designed it.

Timeline Projected into the Future

Ask each participant to share what God revealed to them for their future – to work toward the Mission and Vision that He gave them. A Vision Board can be created as an activity for this lesson to help the participants artistically visualize their future.

Get feedback from others in the class regarding the plans of each person.

Facilitate having the participants evaluate Ministry Opportunities that might come their way against the Mission and Vision He has given them so they can evaluate whether that opportunity would advance or detract from their Mission and Vision.

Close Out with Prayer

Testimony Development

LESSON #22

FACILITATOR'S GUIDE

RESOURCES NEEDED FOR THIS CLASS

- Room Set-up for Testimony Sharing
- Podium

We explored the power of sharing your testimony in Lesson 16, and learned from the Apostle Paul how he tailored his message for the various audiences that he spoke to while sharing his testimony in Lesson 18. Once again, "Testimony" is defined as a declaration by a witness under oath, as that given before a court or deliberative body; evidence in support of a fact or an assertion; or a public declaration regarding a religious experience *(The American Heritage Dictionary of the English Language)*.

This week, we will focus on developing our own testimonies related to our healing from life-controlling sinful behaviors. Over the course of this study, you have been developing your personal timeline (Lesson #6), which is essentially a record of where you have been over the course of your life, and the influences in your life that contributed to your sinful behaviors, and God has been healing areas of your life as you have worked through the exercises and completed the homework assignments.

Every person will be at a different place on the journey towards healing. Some have already experienced complete deliverance from sinful behaviors, and have reached some level of healing from the effects of those life-controlling habits. Others are still struggling, but can identify definite milestones along their path to healing. *There is, therefore, now no condemnation to those who are in Christ Jesus, who do not walk according to the flesh, but according to the Spirit.* (Romans 8:1) Every person has a testimony to share! When we share what God has done for us, He draws people to Himself through our obedience.

Sharing our testimony benefits us as well. It makes what God has done for us so much more real. Thinking and talking about where I came from and how far God has brought me encourages me like nothing else can! Speaking it into the atmosphere seals the healing. It puts Satan on notice that he no longer rules my life. I am now a child of the Most High God and He alone is sanctifying me day by day.

You can use your personal timeline (Lesson #6), along with the Mission and Vision Statements you developed last week to focus the content of your testimony, or use whatever method God shows you to develop the Testimony that He wants you to share. We will share our testimonies when we convene as a group at the completion of this week's homework assignment.

This Week's Memory Verse:

2 Chronicles 16:9a (NKJV) *For the eyes of the Lord run to and fro throughout the whole earth, to show Himself strong on behalf of those whose heart is loyal to Him.*

Review the Memory Verse

- What stood out to you about this Scripture as you were developing your testimony this week?
- What do you think you can do to demonstrate loyalty to God?

Sharing Our Testimonies

Each participant has an opportunity to stand before the group and share their testimony (note the start/stop time to see how close to 3 min they finish).

- Ask for feedback from the audience.
  - ☐ What touched you most about his/her testimony?
  - ☐ What did he/she do well?
  - ☐ How can he/she improve?

- Ask for feedback from the presenter.
  - ☐ How did you feel sharing your testimony?
  - ☐ What do you think you did well?
  - ☐ What do you think you would do differently in the future?

Discussion

Talk about how the participants need to be sensitive to the particular audience where they will be sharing their testimonies and adjust what is said accordingly. The message will be essentially the same, but the delivery may be different.

Lead a discussion regarding how the message might be changed/modified for the following audiences:

- Teens/Pre-teens
- Church Congregation
- Non-church Audiences
- One-on-One meeting

Close Out with Prayer

Personal Plan to Continue Daily Devotional

LESSON #23

FACILITATOR'S GUIDE

RESOURCES NEEDED FOR THIS CLASS

- Ministry Evaluation Forms for completion (located in FORMS section of Facilitator Guide)
- Plan with the group for a final Fellowship next week to formally end the class and collect Evaluation Forms

You have been on quite a journey! Look at how far you have come in your spiritual growth and in your healing from the effects of your life-controlling sinful behaviors, and the development of a deeper intimacy with Jesus. This is just the beginning of the rest of your life, and I know that God has a great plan and purpose for your life.

You have been disciplined in studying the Word of God, as you have completed the homework and in-class exercises over the course of this series. Now, it is time for you to develop your own plan to continue abiding in Jesus Christ and His Word for continual growth and healing. God's Word is powerful and it heals and changes lives. *"For the word of God is living and powerful, and sharper than any two-edged sword, piercing even to the division of soul and spirit, and of joints and marrow, and is a discerner of the thoughts and intents of the heart."* (Hebrews 4:12)

Continued spiritual growth requires discipline. God wants to maintain an intimate and personal relationship with you. He has so much more for your life, and in order for Him to continue to heal your wounds and produce fruit in your life, you have to continue to abide in Him. Jesus says, *"Abide in Me, and I in you. As the branch cannot bear fruit of itself, unless it abides in the vine, neither can you, unless you abide in Me."* (John 15:4) He also promises that if you abide in His Word and meditate on what it teaches, you will be rooted, productive to the Kingdom of God, and prosperous, *"He shall be like a tree planted by the rivers of water, that brings forth its fruit in its season, whose leaf also shall not wither; and whatever he does shall prosper."* (Psalm 1:3)

God will continue to transform your life as He sanctifies you day by day if you remain in His Word, stay connected to Jesus and to other believers. No matter how far you have come over the course of this study or how far you have yet to go in your healing from the effects of your bondage to sin, the Word of God promises change and newness in your life, *"Therefore, if anyone is in Christ, he is a new creation; old things have passed away; behold, all things have become new."* (2 Corinthians 5:17) Walk in the newness of your life in Christ!

May God bless you as you continue your intimate walk with Him. I pray *"that He would grant you, according to the riches of His glory, to be strengthened with might through His Spirit in the inner man, that Christ may dwell in your hearts through faith; that you, being rooted and grounded in love, may be able to comprehend with all the saints what is the width and length and depth and height - to know the love of Christ which passes knowledge; that you may be filled with all the fullness of God."* (Ephesians 3:16-19)

This Week's Memory Verse:

Psalm 119:105 (NKJV) *Your word is a lamp to my feet And a light to my path.*

Note for Facilitator: If possible, it is good to plan a celebration for this final class. Have food and fellowship to celebrate the completion of a journey together.

Review the Memory Verse

What stood out to you about this Scripture as you were developing your plan to stay connected to God and to continue your journey of healing?

Discussion

Go over each day of the homework and ask participants to share their answers to the questions presented. Facilitate sharing.

Encourage participants to maintain contact with each other and with their Accountability Partners over the upcoming weeks and months. Also, encourage them to connect with a Bible-teaching/Bible-believing Church if they are not already connected so they can continue to experience healing and wholeness through the application of the Truth of God's word to their lives.

Remind them that, if they are in Christ, they are a new creation, old things have passed away and all things have become new! (2 Corinthians 5:17) Walk in the newness of life in Christ!

NOTE TO FACILITATOR: If you have feedback or suggestions for improvement to this material, please contact the author: DBarrMinistries@gmail.com

FINAL FELLOWSHIP

This meeting should be a celebration of the journey that everybody has taken together. It is also an opportunity to collect the remaining Final Course Evaluation Forms and an opportunity for the Participants and Accountability Partners to share about their experiences going through this Program.

Forms

All Things New

Participant Registration

Please print legibly and answer every question. Circle response where applicable.

Date: _____

Last Name _____   First Name _____

Street Address _____

City _____   State _____   Zip Code_____

Home # _____   Work # _____   Cell # _____

E-mail Address _____   Date of Birth (mo/day/year)_____

Thank you for your interest in this Ministry. To better serve you during the course of this Bible study, we request that you complete the following questions and bring this form with you on the first day of class. We understand the sensitive nature of these questions and the fact that it may be difficult for you to reveal this information. Please do the best you can to answer the questions truthfully and know that your confidentiality is highly respected.

Have you ever, or do you currently personally experience a life-controlling behavior from which you would like to be free?   Yes   No

If Yes – please explain. Note: if you need more space, continue at the bottom of the second page.

_____

_____

_____

_____

_____

What would you like to get out of your participation in this Discipleship Ministry?

_____

_____

_____

_____

_____

_____

_____

Do you believe that Jesus Christ died to forgive you for your sins?   *Yes   No*

Have you repented of your sins and accepted God's free gift of salvation?   *Yes   No*

If so, when? _____

Continuation from any question above (indicate which question)

_____

_____

_____

_____

_____

_____

_____

_____

_____

ALL THINGS NEW PARTICIPATION REGISTRATION

All Things New

Accountability Partner Application

Thank you for your interest in serving as an Accountability Partner for the All Things New Ministry. Each applicant will be screened by the Ministry Leadership prior to being paired with a person enrolled in the All Things New Discipleship program.

Please print legibly and answer every question on this 2-page application. Circle response where applicable. If you need additional space for any question, please use the second page continuation section.

Date: _____

Last Name _____   First Name _____

Street Address _____

City _____   State _____   Zip Code_____

Home # _____   Work # _____   Cell # _____

E-mail Address _____   Date of Birth (mo/day/year)_____

Have you ever personally experienced a life-controlling sinful behavior?   Yes   No

If yes, please briefly describe your experience and how you overcame it.

_____

_____

_____

_____

_____

Why are you interested in serving as an Accountability Partner?

_____

_____

_____

_____

_____

Current Ministry Involvement

MINISTRY NAME	MY ROLE	DATES OF SERVICE	MINISTRY LEADER phone number

Continuation from any question above (indicate what question)

_____

_____

_____

_____

ALL THINGS NEW ACCOUNTABILITY PARTNER APPLICATION

All Things New
Accountability Partner Rules of Engagement

I understand that I am volunteering to serve as an Accountability/Prayer Partner for a person who is participating in a Bible Study/Discipleship Ministry for people who want to overcome life-controlling sinful behaviors and develop intimacy with Jesus Christ. This ministry, with its weekly group meetings, does not constitute or include any form of professional counseling. I am not required to have any special knowledge about the particular areas of life-controlling behaviors that participants in the ministry may be struggling with. I understand that my application to participate in Ministry as an Accountability Partner will be reviewed by Ministry Leadership prior to my pairing with a person enrolled in the Discipleship program.

All information shared with me by the person I am supporting will be kept confidential, and will not be shared with any person outside of the ministry. Information obtained from a participant will only be shared with the facilitators when it is necessary to learn how best to support him/her. I will immediately contact the ministry facilitators if:

- I believe the person I am supporting is at risk for suicide.
- I believe the person I am supporting intends to harm another person.

I understand that my role is to serve as a Christian friend for a person who desires healing from the effects of life-controlling sinful behaviors.

I WILL

- Talk in person or by telephone with the person I am supporting at a minimum once every 2 weeks

- Provide unconditional non-judgmental love (it is the Holy Spirit's job to convict of sin)

- Listen to his/her story and ask questions to better understand

- Empathize with his/her feelings and stand in a surrogate role of the offender to apologize for hurts he/she has experienced at the hands of others

- Provide a sense of belonging and acceptance of him/her as a child of God right where he/she is without trying to change anything about his/her life

- Provide healthy touch as he/she and I are comfortable (such as hugs or placing my hand on his/her arm or shoulder for a more intimate connection while speaking with him/her)

- Pray for him/her regularly – that God will reveal His truth to him/her

- Contact the ministry facilitators right away when I have questions about how best to support the person I am assigned to

I WILL NOT

- Offer solutions or try to 'fix' his/her situation or circumstances (that is God's role)

- Point out Scriptures that condemn their behavior or use the Bible as a weapon to harm them

- Provide counseling or therapy in any form

- Enter into business dealings with any person who is a part of this ministry

I agree to abide by all of the conditions listed above.

_____   _____

Print name followed by Signature   Date

ALL THINGS NEW ACCOUNTABILITY PARTNER RULES OF ENGAGEMENT

All Things New

Covenant Statement

I understand that I am participating in a Bible Study/Discipleship Ministry facilitated by lay leaders and assisted by volunteer Accountability Partners. This ministry with its weekly group meetings does not constitute or include any form of professional counseling. If at any time I feel that I need additional help for issues that are surfacing, I will speak to my facilitators for a referral for professional counseling in my specific area of need.

Confidentiality: All information shared in the group will be kept confidential. There are certain circumstances in which the facilitator or an Accountability Partner would be compelled to break confidentiality: if we believe you are at risk for suicide or if we believe you intend to harm another person.

Homework Assignments: It is important that participants complete every homework assignment and come to class ready to discuss the lesson for that week. Each week's lesson includes the memorization of a Scripture that relates to the lesson objectives and demonstration of completed homework and Scripture memorization is required each week.

Attendance: A commitment to attend every class and to arrive on time is important as it helps to establish trust; and helps participants to keep up with the class and all of the information shared.

Class Participation: Positive feedback is encouraged in class. We will not allow criticism or put-downs. We are in this group to work on issues pertaining to us, not others. We will share our own insights, experiences, and feelings and will validate and accept the insights, experiences, and feelings of others in the group. We will listen with undivided attention to each person who is speaking, and we will be considerate of the need for all to share, and therefore will not dominate the conversation.

Distractions/Interruptions: We will turn off and put away all cellphones and other electronic devices when we are in class. There will be no texting, or checking social media, or any other distractions of any kind during the 2 hours we meet each week. We will not interrupt others when they are speaking – allow them to completely finish what they are saying.

Avoid Cross Talk: Cross talk is arguing with or verbally attacking another participant, giving advice, responding with criticism, verbally responding to every statement made, or confronting in any way. We must refrain from analyzing, preaching and/or attempting to 'fix' other group members.

No Business Dealings: No members of this ministry may participate in business dealings with any other person who is a part of the ministry.

Accountability Partner Role: Each participant will be paired with an Accountability Partner. Their role is to serve as a Christian friend/mentor to support the person they are assigned to through prayer, encouragement, and friendship. They are to meet with their assigned participant in person or by phone at least once every two weeks. It is also your responsibility as a participant to maintain contact with your Accountability Partner, and to let the Ministry Leaders know if you are unable to stay connected, or if you wish to be reassigned to another Accountability Partner for any reason.

Group Leader Role: This is not a therapy group. The leader is qualified by 'life experiences and/or exposure to training on the issues surrounding bondage to sin,' and not necessarily professional training as a therapist. The leader's role in this group is to create an environment where healing can occur, to support the participant's work towards wholeness, and share their own experience, strength and support.

I understand that any lack of adhering to any of the above stated requirements will be addressed by the Leader(s) and/or by the Group.

Signed: _____ Date: _____

Printed Name: _____

Leader: _____ Date: _____

All Things New
Session Progress Report

Please read each question and honestly evaluate yourself by using the following scale:

1= All/Majority of the time   2 = Sometimes   3 = Rarely   4 = Never

Name _____ *Date:* _____

		Rating
1.	I spend daily time with the Lord (through prayer, reading God's Word, etc.)	_____
2.	I memorize the weekly Scripture verses	_____
3.	I complete the homework assignments	_____
4.	I maintain contact with my accountability partner	_____
5.	I have encouraged someone outside the ministry with what I have learned	_____
6.	I arrive at class on time	_____
7.	I participate in class discussions	_____
8.	I attend weekly church services in addition to this Ministry	_____
9.	I am applying what I am learning in this Ministry to my life	_____

Questions

1. Where do you see yourself going/doing after completing All Things New?

_____

_____

_____

_____

_____

_____

2. Have you grown since you have been in All Things New? If so, how? If not, why?

_____

_____

_____

_____

_____

ALL THINGS NEW SESSION PROGRESS REPORT

For Facilitators Only:

		Rating
1.	Participant participates in class on a regular basis	_____
2.	Participant completes homework	_____
3.	Participant has memorized Scriptures	_____
4.	Participant has displayed some form of growth	_____

Comments:

_____

_____

_____

_____

_____

_____

_____

All Things New
Accountability Partner Evaluation

Please read each question and evaluate your accountability partner by using the following scale:

1= All/Majority of the time   2 = Sometimes   3 = Rarely   4 = Never

Accountability Partner's Name _____ *Date:* _____

		Rating
1.	I meet with him/her by phone or face to face at least once every 2 weeks	_____
2.	He/she communicates in a non-judgmental way	_____
3.	He/she listens well	_____
4.	He/she is easy to talk to	_____
5.	He/she prays for me	_____
6.	I feel like he/she cares about me	_____
7.	He/she refers to Scriptures condemning my behavior	_____

What does he/she do well?

_____

_____

_____

_____

_____

_____

What could he/she do better?

_____

_____

_____

_____

_____

_____

_____

_____

Please describe any concerns or anything else you would like to share about your Accountability Partner.

_____

_____

_____

_____

_____

_____

_____

_____

_____

_____

ALL THINGS NEW ACCOUNTABILITY PARTNER EVALUATION

All Things New
Facilitator Evaluation

Evaluate each facilitator in the columns provided

Leader's Name _____ *Date:* _____

1 – Never   2 – Rarely   3 - Sometimes   4 - Most of the Time   5 - Always

Questions	Rating
1. In your observation, is this leader committed to the Ministry?	_____
2. Is he/she prepared for the lessons?	_____
3. Is the lesson discussion intriguing or creative?	_____
4. Does he/she refer to the Bible throughout the lesson?	_____
5. Are the All Things New sessions helping to meet your needs?	_____
6. Have the lessons been real and applicable to your life?	_____
7. Does he/she take the time to hear what the participants want to share?	_____
8. Would you recommend All Things New to a friend?	_____
9. Does he/she listen to what you have to say?	_____
10. Does he/she hold you accountable for completing the lessons?	_____
11. Does he/she hold you accountable for knowing your memory scriptures?	_____
12. Does he/she hold you accountable for attending class?	_____
13. Does he/she monopolize the conversation too much?	_____
14. Does she/he maintain confidentiality and create a safe place to share?	_____
15. Does he/she start and stop class on time?	_____

Suggestions/Improvements/Comments/Complaints

ALL THINGS NEW FACILITATOR EVALUATION

All Things New
Final Evaluation

Please read each question and honestly evaluate yourself by using the following scale:

1= All/Majority of the time   2 = Sometimes   3 = Rarely   4 = Never

Name _____ Date: _____

		Rating
1.	I spend daily time with the Lord (through prayer, reading God's Word, etc.)	_____
2.	I memorize the weekly Scripture verses	_____
3.	I complete the homework assignments	_____
4.	I maintain contact with my accountability partner	_____
5.	I have encouraged someone outside the ministry with what I have learned	_____
6.	I arrive at class on time	_____
7.	I participate in class discussions	_____
8.	I attend weekly church services in addition to this Ministry	_____
9.	I am applying what I am learning in this Ministry to my life	_____

Questions

1. Where do you see yourself going now that you have completed All Things New?

_____

_____

_____

_____

2. Have you grown since you have been in All Things New? If so, how? If not, why?

_____

_____

_____

_____

_____

3. What would you recommend needs to be changed about this Ministry to make it more effective?

_____

_____

_____

_____

_____

Testimony – *How has this Ministry impacted your life?*

_____

_____

_____

_____

_____

_____

ALL THINGS NEW FINAL EVALUATION

All Things New

Accountability Partner's
Evaluation of the All Things New Ministry

Please read each question and evaluate each one by using the following scale:

1= All/Majority of the time   2 = Sometimes   3 = Rarely   4 = Never

Name of ATN Participant Assigned to _____ *Date:* _____

My Interaction with ATN Participant Assigned to Support	**Rating**
I meet with him/her by phone or face to face at least once every 2 weeks	_____
He/she responds well to my suggestions/encouragement	_____
He/she is easy to talk to	_____
I am being enriched by my support of him/her	_____
I am growing spiritually by supporting him/her	_____
He/she is growing spiritually as a result of this Ministry	_____
I feel like he/she values my support	_____

My Interaction with ATN Ministry Leaders and the Ministry as a Whole	**Rating**
I have the support I need for my role as Accountability Partner	_____
They are accessible/available when I have questions/concerns	_____
They are committed to supporting the participants in this Ministry	_____
I feel valued for my participation in this Ministry	_____
The periodic Accountability Partner meetings are helpful	_____
Participating in this Ministry is a valuable/productive use of my time	_____

What aspects of this Ministry are going well?

_____

_____

_____

_____

In what areas of this Ministry is there room for improvement?

_____

_____

_____

_____

Based on your participation in this Ministry so far, would you agree to support another person going through this Ministry in the future?   Yes _____   No _____

If you answered No, please explain why:

_____

_____

_____

_____

Please describe any concerns or anything else you would like to share about your experience in this Ministry so far.

_____

_____

_____

_____

_____

ALL THINGS NEW ACCOUNTABILITY PARTNER'S EVALUATION OF THE ALL THINGS NEW MINISTRY

All Things New
Weekly Notes

Leader Taking Notes _____ *Date* _____

Participant Worship Leader _____

Participant Name	Memory	Scripture Homework	Complete Notes

Notes/Concerns/Prayer Requests:

_____

_____

_____

_____

_____

_____

Individual Lessons

The Word is Life

LESSON #1

CLASSROOM DISCUSSION

Bible Facts

1. The _____ _____ of the Bible (_____ Old Testament and _____ New Testament) were written:

   • By more than _____ _____ inspired by _____
   • Over a period of approximately _____ years

The Power of God's Word to Transform Lives

2. Scripture is profitable for _____, _____, _____, and _____ in righteousness (2 Timothy 3:16-17)

3. The Word of God is _____ and _____ (Hebrews 4:12-13)

4. The Word of God is a _____ of the _____ and _____ of the heart. (Hebrews 4:12-13)

5. The Word will_____your life if you_____ what you learn to your life. (James 1:21-25)

6. We are to be _____ of the Word and not _____only (James 1:21-25)

The Enemy's Lies vs. God's Truth

LESSON #2

CLASSROOM DISCUSSION

The Enemy Has Been Trying to Destroy You

1. Your _____, the devil, walks about like a _____ _____ seeking someone to devour. (1 Peter 5:8)

2. Our _____ is the _____ of the brethren, who stands before _____ day and night pointing out what we have done wrong. (Rev 12:10)

3. The _____ desires to _____ us as _____, but Jesus _____ for us that our _____ may not fail. (Luke 22:31)

God Loves You

4. Before God _____ you in your mother's womb, He _____ you, and He _____ you. (Jeremiah 1:5, and Psalm 139:13)

5. _____ things work together for _____ to those who _____ _____ and are _____ _____ according to His _____. For those He _____ He also _____ to be conformed to the _____ of Jesus. (Romans 8:28-29)

6. _____ knows the _____ He thinks towards you, thoughts of _____ and not _____ – to give you a _____ and a _____. (Jeremiah 29:11)

7. You are to be _____ with might through _____ in the _____ man, that _____ may dwell in your heart through _____, being _____ and _____ in love you may be able to comprehend

what is the _____ and _____ and _____ and _____

– to _____ the love of _____. (Eph 3:16-19)

Freedom in Truth

CLASSROOM DISCUSSION

1. Jesus does not _____ sinners – He _____ them. (John 8:1-11)

2. When we encounter Jesus and our _____ are exposed to Him – he _____ our _____ and tells us to go and _____ _____ _____. (John 8:11)

3. If we _____ our _____ He is faithful and just to _____ us our _____ and _____ us from all _____. (1 John 1:9)

4. Jesus reacts to our _____ with _____ and _____. (Luke 7:44-50)

5. _____ in Jesus is what saves us and gives us _____. (Luke 7:50)

Testimony Sharing

- When did you first experience a life-controlling issue that you are not proud of (how old were you)?
- What do you think is the cause of your behavior?

Hearing God's Voice

EXERCISE – PART I

		L	O U	G D	S	D	L	
G	O L	D R		V U		O E	G R	
	U	V	D	G O E	G U U			L

Hearing God's Voice

LESSON #4

EXERCISE – PART II

Rules: Fill in the grid so that every row, every column, and every 3x3 box contains the letters named under the board. The iagonal will contain an English word. There is only 1 solution for the puzzle.

		L		G		D		
		O		D				
G		U			S		L	
	O	D		V			G	
		R				O		
	L			U		E	R	
	U		D		G			L
				O	U			
		V		E	U			

Letters: DEGLORSUV

Hearing God's Voice

EXERCISE – SOLUTION

O	S	L	E	G	V	D	U	R
R	V	U	O	D	L	S	E	G
G	D	E	U	R	S	V	L	O
S	O	D	R	V	E	L	G	U
U	E	R	G	L	D	O	S	V
V	L	G	S	U	O	E	R	D
E	U	O	D	S	G	R	V	L
L	R	S	V	O	U	G	D	E
D	G	V	L	E	R	U	O	S

Letters: DEGLORSUV

Hearing God's Voice

LESSON #4

CLASSROOM DISCUSSION

God 'speaks' to His children in a variety of ways:

1. God _____ to us through _____. (Romans 1:19-20)

2. God _____ to us through the _____ _____. (Romans 10:14; 1 Corinthians 1:21; Acts 10:42).

3. God _____ to us through _____ and _____. (Exodus 4:1-9; Acts 4:22; Acts 5:12; Hebrews 2:1-4).

4. God _____ to us when we _____ Him. (John 4:24; James 4:6; Acts 17:24-25).

5. God _____ to us through _____. (Acts 16:16-34).

6. God _____ to us through his _____. (1 Tim 3:16; James 1:21-25).

Prayer – Communicating with God

LESSON #5

CLASSROOM DISCUSSION

Our Prayers Move God on our Behalf

1. God will _____ His _____ towards us when we pray. (Psalm 116:2; Psalm 17:6; Psalm 10:17; 1 Peter 3:12)

2. God will sometimes _____ our prayers before we _____ _____. (Isaiah 65:24)

3. God _____ the prayers of the _____. (Psalm 22:24; Jonah 2:2,7)

4. When we _____ ourselves, and _____, and _____ from our _____ ways, God will _____ us. (2 Chronicles 7:14)

Power of Praying Scripture Back to God

5. You can be _____ that God will _____ what He has said in His _____. (Isaiah 55:11)

6. When God has _____ something specific in Scripture we can be _____ that _____ will answer that prayer. (Deuteronomy 30:2-5/Nehemiah 1:9)

Jesus Intercedes (Prays) on our Behalf

7. Jesus _____ for _____ believers to be _____ with Him. (John 17:20-26)

8. Jesus _____ on our behalf as our _____ _____ (Hebrews 7:25; 1 John 2:1)

9. _____ is at the _____ _____ of the Father _____ on our behalf. (Romans 8:34)

Fall of Man – Root Causes of Sin

LESSON #6

CLASSROOM DISCUSSION

Abandonment

Genesis 21:8-16

Lies/Deceit and Trickery

Genesis Chapter 27

Sexual Abuse

2 Samuel Chapter 13

TIMELINE/ROOT CAUSE EXERCISE

This exercise is for your eyes only. It will not be turned in to the facilitators. However, we will discuss the results of the exercise in class, and recommend that you share what you are learning about yourself with your Accountability Partner. Write what you feel comfortable writing – to help you remember for processing and discussion later.

You will be creating a timeline of your life from birth to now as if you were preparing to write your autobiography. The purpose of this exercise is to help you:

- Identify the significant things/events that have occurred in your lifetime (good and bad, joyful and painful) that cause you to think and behave the way you do;
- Recognize patterns of behavior in your life; and
- See how it all fits together to make you the person you have become (warts and all).

Add to your timeline as God continues to reveal things to you over the next several weeks.

Instructions for Completion

1. Notes about my relationship with my mother and other significant women in my life from childhood until now.

2. Notes about my relationship with my father and other significant men in my life from childhood until now.

3. Significant things that happened to me over my lifetime (both good and bad). Note your age at each milestone.

4. How I have felt about myself from childhood until now.

5. My history of drug/alcohol use (earliest exposure, and most recent).

6. Anything else God is revealing to me about my life.

Some Possible Root Causes of my Sinful Behaviors

1. Notes about my relationship with my mother and other significant women in my life from childhood until now.

_____

_____

_____

2. Notes about my relationship with my father and other significant men in my life from childhood until now.

_____

_____

_____

_____

3. Significant things that happened to me over my lifetime (both good and bad). Note your age at each milestone.

_____

_____

_____

_____

4. How I have felt about myself from childhood until now.

_____

_____

_____

_____

5. My history of drug/alcohol use (earliest exposure and most recent).

_____

_____

_____

_____

6. Anything else God is revealing to me about my life.

_____

_____

_____

_____

_____

Timeline

For this exercise, you will use the next page to construct your own timeline.

Example

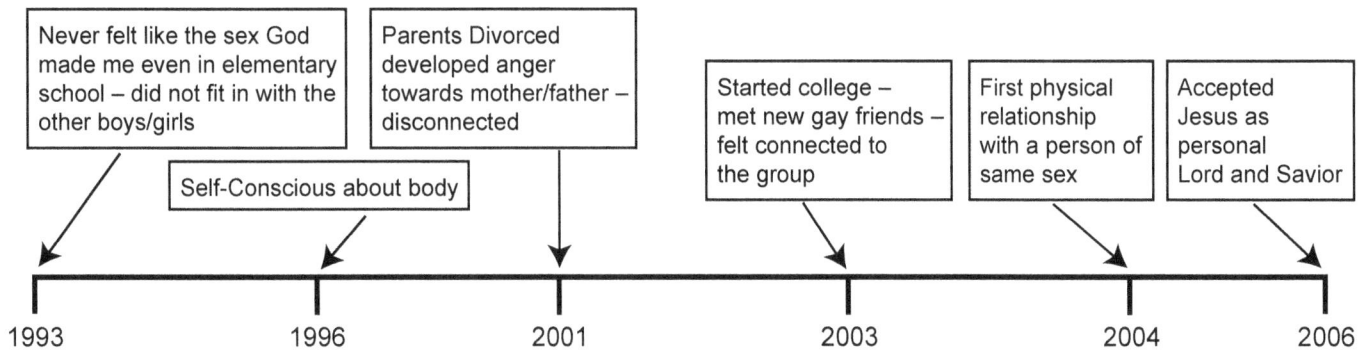

Never felt like the sex God made me even in elementary school – did not fit in with the other boys/girls	Parents Divorced developed anger towards mother/father – disconnected		Started college – met new gay friends – felt connected to the group	First physical relationship with a person of same sex	Accepted Jesus as personal Lord and Savior
	Self-Conscious about body				
1993	1996	2001	2003	2004	2006

Feelings (example for a girl)

1993   *I never felt connected to other girls when I was young; I hung out with the boys and only played with them*

1996   *The kids in school made fun of me because I had a flat chest and didn't develop like the other girls. I felt embarrassed and ashamed about my body.*

2001   *When my parents divorced, I hated my mother because I felt that she didn't try to stay with dad. She wasn't there for me and I decided I didn't want to be like her.*

2003   *I met new friends in college that were gay; they were nice to me and accepted me for who I was. I finally felt like I belonged.*

2004   *My first sexual relationship with a woman was exhilarating. I felt like she really loved me and accepted me for who I am.*

2006   *Confused – want to line my life up with the Word of God but don't know how.*

(Note this example is from the author's life and will likely be very different from your experiences)

TIMELINE/ROOT CAUSES AND MILESTONES

MAJOR MILESTONES AND FEELINGS

Fall of Man – Root Causes of Sin

LESSON #6

CLASSROOM DISCUSSION

Abandonment

Genesis 21:8-16

Lies/Deceit and Trickery

Genesis Chapter 27

Sexual Abuse

2 Samuel Chapter 13

Forgiveness

CLASSROOM DISCUSSION

What Forgiveness is and What it is Not

(Adapted from Resolving Everyday Conflict, Ken Sande & Kevin Johnson, (Baker Books 2011) © Peacemaker Ministries).

1. Forgiveness is NOT _____ (Isaiah 43:25)

2. Forgiveness is NOT _____ (Psalm 32:5)

What Forgiveness IS

3. Forgiveness IS a _____ _____ (Romans 5:8)

4. Forgiveness IS _____ and _____ be _____ (Romans 5:8)

5. Forgiveness IS an _____ _____ (Matthew 18:21-22)

There are Two Components of Forgiveness

6. The First Component of Forgiveness is the _____ Component (Romans 12:18)

7. The Second Component of Forgiveness is the _____ or _____ component. (Matthew 18:15)

4 Promises of Forgiveness

1. I will not _____ on this incident

2. I will not _____ this incident _____ and _____ it _____ you

3. I will not _____ to _____ about this incident

4. I will not allow this incident to _____ _____ us or _____ our personal relationship

Forgiveness

IN-CLASS EXERCISE

Choose one person that you identified this week during your homework exercises that you have not yet forgiven for what they did or failed to do. Write their name here: _____

In the space below, write a letter to God expressing your "attitude of forgiveness" - your willingness to forgive that person regardless of whether they have asked for forgiveness or not, or even if they have passed away and are no longer alive. Completely release that person from the offense(s) in your letter to God. Be specific (these letters will not be shared with anyone unless you choose to share them).

_____

_____

_____

_____

_____

_____

_____

_____

_____

_____

_____

_____

After you express your complete forgiveness of that person, write a prayer of blessing over the life of the person who has offended you. Pray that God will bless them (Matthew 5:44). Also pray and ask God to heal your heart from the pain of the offense.

My prayer of blessing:

_____

_____

_____

_____

_____

_____

_____

_____

_____

_____

_____

_____

_____

_____

_____

Sexual Integrity

LESSON #8

CLASSROOM DISCUSSION

Sexual Integrity and Sexual Impurity

1. does not tempt us to sin, we are tempted by _____ when we are away by our own _____ and enticed. (James 1:13-14)

2. _____ , not _____ we are _____ to sin, God will make a way of escape for us. (1 Corinthians 10:13)

3. We sin against God _____ , when we look _____ with our eyes at another person. (Matthew 5:27-28)

4. Every sin that a man does is outside the body, but he who commits _____ sins against his own _____ . (1 Corinthians 6:18)

5. Whoever   sin is a to sin. (John 8:34)

The Mind and the Heart

6. Cast down arguments and every _____ _____ that exalts itself against the knowledge of God, bringing every _____ into _____ to the _____ of Christ. (2 Corinthians 10:5)

7. To be _____ minded is _____, but to be _____ minded is _____ and peace. (Romans 8:6)

8. We must set our minds on things _____ not on things on the _____. (Colossians 3:2)

9. Guard your _____ by _____ on the _____ to protect yourself from sexual immorality. (Proverbs 4:23, Matthew 15:19, Psalm 119:11)

Final Thoughts

10. If we _____ our sins, His is faithful and just to _____ us our sins and to _____ us from all unrighteousness. (1 John 1:9)

Spiritual Warfare

CLASSROOM DISCUSSION

Primary weapons of the enemy – how he wages battle against us

1. _____

2. _____

3. _____

How are the weapons of the devil used to attack a person (particularly a Christian) in the area of sin and how do we fight back?

Deception – "I have experienced negative things in my life and therefore, I am not loved."

_____ (Jeremiah 31:3)

_____ (John 3:16, Isaiah 43:18-19)

Temptation – to believe that whatever the enemy is dangling before me as an unholy temptation is what I need and want.

How do you combat the temptation to fall for the trap of the enemy?

_____ (James 4:7)

Accusation – if you submit to the temptation and go where you have no business going, the devil then accuses you and condemns you for your sin.

Which piece of the Armor of God should you use to combat the accusations of the enemy for your sin?

_____ of Faith.

What should you do when you fall into sin?

_____ and ask for forgiveness. (1 John 1:9, John 3:17)

Do not be afraid of the attacks of the enemy.

You have the _____ to cast out demons. (Luke 10:19)

The Heart

CLASSROOM DISCUSSION

1. We are _____ when we trust in _____ to give us strength and allow our _____ to _____ from God. (Jeremiah 17:5)

2. We are to _____ from _____. (1 Corinthians 10:14)

   1 Corinthians 10:14 - *Therefore, my beloved, flee from idolatry.*

Hardening of the Heart

Some people, as a result of past hurts in their lives, have allowed their hearts to turn to stone as a defense mechanism to protect them from further hurt.

3. God will take the heart of _____ out of your flesh and give you a new heart of _____. (Ezekiel 36:26)

   Discuss Ephesians 3:16-19.

Our Authority in Christ to Rout Demons

LESSON #11

CLASSROOM DISCUSSION

1. The _____ we fight and the _____ we use are not of this world, they are _____. (2 Corinthians 10:3-5)

2. To demolish the _____ that keep us in bondage to sin, we have to _____ God and change our _____. (2 Corinthians 10:3-5)

Daniel 3:1-30 – Notes:

3. We are to _____ _____ as a good soldier, _____ to Jesus Christ. (2 Timothy 2:3-4)

4. I am God's _____ and have already _____ the enemy because I have God in me and therefore I am _____ than the enemy who is in the world. (1 John 4:4)

Forgiveness – Part II

LESSON #12

CLASSROOM DISCUSSION

1. If Jesus makes you _____ from your sin, you are _____ indeed. (John 8:36)

2. We are _____ by the blood of Jesus and are granted _____ of our sins according to the riches of His _____. (Ephesians 1:7)

3. While Jesus stands ready to forgive us of our sins, there are some prerequisites to receiving God's forgiveness. What do you suppose they are?

   • _____ (Matthew 9:13)

   • _____ (1 John 1:9)

   • _____ (1 John 5:14-15, Matthew 21:22)

4. When Jesus forgives our sins, He chooses _____ to _____ our _____. (Hebrews 8:12)

5. God stands ready to _____ us, and He is _____ and _____ towards us. (Psalm 86:4-5)

6. Nothing can _____ us from the _____ of God. (Romans 8:38-39)

Prayer Blockers
Possible Reasons Why Our Prayers are Not Answered by God

LESSON #13

IN-CLASS SMALL GROUP EXERCISE

We can learn a lot from the example left for us by others who are written about in the Bible. Look up the Scriptures identified below and make a list of the various reasons why God did not answer the prayers of people who prayed to him.

Scripture Reference	Hindrance(s) to Effective Prayer
Deuteronomy 1:45 1 Samuel 14:37 1 Samuel 28:6	
Proverbs 1:24-28	
Proverbs 28:9	
Isaiah 1:15 Isaiah 59:3	
Isaiah 59:2 Micah 3:4 John 9:31 Psalm 66:18	
Zechariah 7:11-13	
James 1:6,7	

James 4:3	
2 Corinthians 12:8 Exodus 33:20 Ezekiel 20:3	
Hosea 5:1-7 Luke 18:11, 12, 14	
Isaiah 1:2-20	
Proverbs 21:13	
Jeremiah 14:10,12	
Proverbs 1:24, 25, 28	
Jeremiah 11:11-14 Ezekiel 8:15-18	
Job 27:8,9	
Job 35:12,13	

Exposing the Pain and Glorifying God

IN-CLASS EXERCISE

Take 3-5 minutes and think about the first time you experienced a life-controlling sinful behavior.

Write down what triggered it, what someone else did, what you did, how it made you feel, and what you now know about the root cause(s) of these feelings:

After knowing all you know now about what that experience opened up in your life, how would you warn a friend who reveals to you that he/she is experiencing a similar situation?

Pair up with a partner and share your testimony (5 minutes for each person to share).

Tailoring Your Message
for the Listener

IN-CLASS EXERCISE

Identify one family member or friend who you know is not saved (has not accepted Jesus as their personal Lord and Savior):

Suppose that person walks up to you and asks you why you believe in Jesus? What difference has it made in your life? What would you say to them? Jot down some notes below:

We will have an opportunity to share with someone else in the group who will serve as a surrogate (stand-in) for the person you identified above.

After sharing:

- How did it feel to share your testimony in this way?
- Do you feel you could do this if that person came up to you and asked you the question tomorrow?
- What can you do to strengthen your testimony?

Testimony Development and Sharing

PURPOSE

The purpose of our testimony development is to practice sharing our testimonies of deliverance and healing and of what God has done in our lives so far. Don't worry or feel discouraged if you have not reached a point in your journey where you feel like you are completely free from same-sex attraction! We are all at different stages of our healing. Focus on what God has done in your life to bring you to where you are right now. Something has occurred in your life that has brought you to the point to seek out this ministry – and kept you coming back…that is your testimony.

GUIDELINES FOR TESTIMONY DEVELOPMENT/DELIVERY

Each person will have three (3) minutes to share their testimony, which should follow this general outline:

1. How was your life before - what happened?

2. How did God impact your life for change, deliverance, healing?

3. What is different about your life now?

It is best to write out your testimony, considering who your audience is (helps determine what parts of your story to tell and what parts to leave out). Don't worry about length on the first draft. After you finish, read it out loud, and time yourself from start to finish. You will then know how much needs to be cut out to bring it down to 3 minutes. The finished written transcript should be about 350 words for a 3-minute testimony.

Once you have it down on paper – practice – practice – practice (with a timer – like the free one available at: http://www.online-stopwatch.com/) and refine it until you are satisfied.